Love
is
Now

BOOKS BY PETER E. GILLQUIST . . .
Love Is Now
Let's Quit Fighting About the Holy Spirit
The Physical Side of Being Spiritual

Fresh new insight
into

Love
IS
Now

By Peter E. Gillquist

Foreword by Sherwood E. Wirt

**ZONDERVAN
PUBLISHING HOUSE** OF THE ZONDERVAN CORPORATION
GRAND RAPIDS, MICHIGAN 49506

Love Is Now
© 1970, 1978 by Zondervan Publishing House
Grand Rapids, Michigan
Revised Edition, First printing 1978

Seventh revised printing August 1982

Library of Congress Cataloging in Publication Data

Gillquist, Peter E
    Love is now.

    Includes bibliographical references.
    1.   Christian life—1960-   I.   Title.
BV4501.2.G5115   1978   248'.4   77-17867
ISBN 0-310-36941-X

Unless otherwise stated, Old Testament quotations are from the King James Version,
and New Testament quotations are from *The New American Standard Bible — New
Testament*, copyright © 1963 by THE LOCKMAN FOUNDATION. Used by special per-
mission.

Printed in the United States of America

CONTENTS

Foreword to First Edition

In May, 1963, when Evangelist Billy Graham came to Paris for a campaign, the French magazine *Arts* devoted several satirical columns to his appearance, titling its report, "La voix de Dieu a l'accent de Minneapolis." Four weeks later the first *Decision* magazine School of Christian Writing opened under the auspices of The Billy Graham Evangelistic Association — in Minneapolis.

In launching the school we did not presume to claim that the voice of God had a Minneapolis accent, but we did venture the hope that out of the annual event would come a band of young, fresh, spirited authors who would speak for God to this generation — in an evangelistic accent. We looked for talented writers who would interpret the saving gospel of Jesus Christ in the idiom of a new generation.

Among the hundreds of young Christians who have attended the school during the past six years, Peter Gillquist was unforgettable. Tall, blond, Scandinavian, eloquent, Peter brought with him a national reputation as a campus evangelist. For him it was a homecoming, for he holds diplomas from Washburn High School and the University of Minnesota. During our days together God gave him a vision of the power of the printed word to win men.

I am excited about this, Gillquist's first book, not just because it breathes a captivating style, but because it carries the authentic stamp of the man and his tremendous zeal for Christ. The message he proclaims is one to which his contemporaries will respond; of that I have no doubt. It carries the flair and tang of a generation that is trailblazing for the Lord. May God give it a great run, and prove Himself anew to us all.

SHERWOOD ELIOT WIRT

Preface to Revised Edition

By all rights, the signature of authorship for this book should be corporate. The theme for its contents emerged from the hearts of five of us who met together over seven o'clock breakfast during the summer of 1967. The seeds God planted within us during those weeks have since sprung up into newness of life for us all.

We desired that the truths God began to show us that summer would somehow be made available to all who cared to share them — not because it was we who had learned them, for so many others had also learned them in ages past, but *because our lives were changed.*

Since the first edition of *Love Is Now* was published in 1970, I have experienced spiritual growth in a basic area which I trust will be evident to you who read this second edition. I have learned this: a specific *garden* is needed for the people of God to grow in, a place where His love and grace can be most fully known. That garden is the church of Jesus Christ.

Too little of this garden, too little of the kingdom of God, the family of God, the government of God came through in the earlier edition. Therefore, while the priceless message of the unconditional love and forgiveness of Jesus Christ remains unchanged in this new edition, there's a heightened emphasis upon the glorious place where it all is supposed to happen: the church.

My special thanks to John and Marjorie Dold of Wilmette, Illinois, for handling the typing and the duplication of the first manuscript, and to Martha Ann Bland of Grand Junction, Tennessee, for the same enthusiastic assistance on the second. Two men consistently helped me overcome my cold feet as I began writing: Dr. Sherwood Wirt, formerly editor of *Decision* magazine, and Dr. Robert K. DeVries, executive vice-president of Zondervan Publishing House. I express my sincere gratitude to them for keeping me moving.

Then, there is a lovely lady who has done more to help me than either she or I will ever know. As I wrote, she prayed. Thank you, "Grandma Mac," for your unseen help. Other friends made constructive comments on the manuscript which formed a pattern to guide final corrections. I tried, whenever possible, to incorporate their suggestions into the text.

My wife and sweetheart, Marilyn, above and beyond her literary observations, consistently provides that "home atmosphere" in which I write. Thanks, Baby, for just being you.

If these pages reveal to you but a portion of the love and peace God has brought into my own life, my purpose will have been fully met.

PETER E. GILLQUIST

Love
is
Now

For I am confident of this very thing, that He who began a good work in you will perfect it until the day of Jesus Christ.

Philippians 1:6

1. Beginnings

It was springtime; the year was 1959. As we looked across from the east bank, it was good to see the Mississippi flowing again at full force.

The campus itself was coming back to life from its wintry sleep. Weekly rehearsals for Campus Carnival would soon change to three times a week, and finally, every night. The Carnival was a big event at the University of Minnesota, especially if you belonged to a fraternity or sorority.

Things were going too well. There was always plenty to do to keep a person from really facing himself. The Carnival was just a part of the activity. House parties on the weekends, late-night bull sessions, intramural athletic events. For me, even bad things like grades and classes were no longer a threat. I seemed to have the academic scene analyzed well enough to at least pull Bs and Cs — and what more could a college junior ask for? In addition, I had just become pinned to a lovely green-eyed blonde and was convinced she was the "one" for me. I was active on the campus, active in the house and had plenty of money as a result of two well-paying part-time jobs. My first car, a spotless 1951 Buick Roadmaster named Charles, was by far the slickest thing on campus. There was just one hang-up: no purpose to it all. But why get sidetracked with peripheral inconsequentials like purpose and meaning when there was a whole big life to live?

The invasion of this self-erected security shield came on a Monday evening that spring. It was dinner time and chapter night which meant all the men in the fraternity house were together for the evening meeting. Just as we were finishing dinner, our president announced that we would be hosting a panel of four men for a half-hour after-dinner discussion before our chapter meeting began. Then the bomb was dropped — the subject announced was "Christianity."

My first inclination was to quietly slip out. We had never had a Christian meeting in my two years as a member of Sigma Alpha Epsilon, and I, for one, did not wish to begin. It was not that I was opposed to religion. My thought was, why flog a dead horse? God and I already had a smooth-working relationship: I didn't bother Him and He didn't bother me.

After dinner about seventy of us gathered in the living room to hear what these men had to say. I had pictured in my mind's eye four little old fellows with bony index fingers aimed at me who would get after us for moral misdemeanors. They'd be wearing baggy suits, yellowed white shirts, and have gravy stains on their hand-painted Hawaiian neckties. Their eyeglasses would be as thick as the bottoms of Coke bottles, and their beady stares would come through even stronger as a result. I was, without question, psychologically "up" for their presentation!

The first man to speak was an exchange student from India. He was working for his double doctorate at the university. He had come to this country as a Hindu, and his desire, he said, was not just to study in America but also to investigate Christianity. He began by telling us how he had systematically and objectively considered all of the eleven living religions of the world and had discovered that the founder of just one, namely Jesus of Nazareth, had ever claimed to be God. He studied the life and teachings of Jesus Christ and terminated his quest by a personal surrender of his life to Him. After his commitment to Christ, his parents rejected him and ceased to send him monetary aid. For two years he lived by faith, and God met every need he had.

We, listening, were amazed. I doubt that any of us had ever heard anyone talk so intimately of a relationship with God as this young Indian did that evening.

The next person who spoke was not of the same intellectual heritage as the first. In fact, he was the co-captain of our football team. But as he stood and shared with us his relationship to Christ, it was apparent that he, too, possessed the same quality of life as did the first speaker.

By the time the meeting had ended, most of us concluded that either these men had what we wanted or else they were just plain deluded — one of the two.

A couple of days later I had coffee with one of the men on the panel at the Varsity Cafe on campus. He related in detail how I could experience a true and meaningful walk with God. I knew it made sense, but I felt I needed time. I asked Ray if he would mind stopping by the house on Wednesday evenings just so we could talk further. (I recall that I always invited two or three of the fraternity brothers to be on hand just so the conversation would not get too personal.) We began studying the Bible.

During the third or fourth week that we had met together on

this basis, I spotted a passage in the Gospel of John which captured my imagination. Jesus was speaking, and He said, "I am come that they might have life, and that they might have it more abundantly."[1] The phrase "more abundantly" was what hit me. Somehow I had surmised that if I were to become a Christian everything would first have to go all wrong. Then, from the depths of isolation and fear, I could cry out for my Maker. It is true that some people come to God that way. I was not one of them.

Overtly, as I have stated, everything was going extremely well. Life, I felt, was already abundant. But here was this thing Jesus had promised in the way of *more* abundance. Naturally it was appealing. This could well be the answer to my purpose gap. I told Ray I did not want to be pushed, but that I was interested. (There was a desire to respond to God all on my own, so that Ray could not say he had persuaded me to pray with him.) That night as I climbed into my top bunk in the second-floor dorm of the fraternity, I pulled the covers over my head and invited Jesus Christ to enter my life and do with it as He pleased.

I guess I trusted Him partly as my Savior and partly as my Hero. What spoke to me at that point was not so much His death for my sins as His promise to give me a better life. I really had no concept of heaven or hell. A relationship with Jesus was a right now kind of thing. And I did believe that if I would ask Him to enter into my life He would do it.

The next morning I woke up with a new awareness of His being a part of me. The feeling I had was one I had had before, only far more intense. It's the feeling that usually comes after you do something you know is right. I sensed God was pleased, too.

The rest of the spring that year came off as planned. We didn't place in Campus Carnival, but some of the guys did get pinned to some of the girls in the sorority with which we teamed up for the show. The fraternity sponsored a picnic in May, but this time *I* was the one who helped carry a few of the *other* guys into waiting cars when it was over. A new concern for other people, such as I had not experienced since I was a small child, began to express itself.

Of great encouragement was the fact that my pinmate (who is now my beloved wife) had met Christ that same spring, a few weeks ahead of me. I had some catching up to do. Before my turning to God, Marilyn and I had discussed at length her own newly acquired sincerity for going God's way. She was almost bewildered when I received Christ because I had indicated no real interest whatever in the Christian life. After I admitted to her that I had trusted in Christ as my own, we would talk regularly about Him.

In a few weeks school was out, and I was off to Fort Riley, Kansas, for six weeks of military training with the ROTC unit from Minnesota. Letters from Marilyn kept me stoked spiritually, to the point that I began to share with a few of the men at camp my new relationship with Christ.

Back in Minneapolis later in the summer, my thinking began to jell with regard to God's life plan for me. First, I was deeply impressed by a movie shown at Marilyn's church on the life of Peter Marshall, for it was through this film that God called me as a worker in the body of Christ. Second, at a conference just outside the Twin Cities late in August, I heard a message describing the in-filling of the Holy Spirit, and I felt that through understanding the fact of His life within, my life would never again be the same. A week later, Marilyn and I served as counselors at a church camp in northern Minnesota. As we talked that week with others about knowing Jesus Christ in a personal way, many responded, including some of the other counselors.

I returned to campus in the fall and enrolled for the first quarter of my senior year. The summer had been a good experience. The personalness of the Holy Spirit had become a reality for the first time, and I sensed a new strength and willingness to obey God. From that time on, I never questioned God's presence within me.

But even in light of what I had learned, things began to go wrong in this matter of being filled with the Holy Spirit. I leaked! Introspection set in, and I began to wonder if little things I was doing would turn Him off. I started to develop a grand capacity for looking inward at myself, rather than looking upward toward Christ.

A cardinal point of my personal Christian doctrine at this early stage concerned the matter of sin. To me, being filled with the Holy Spirit meant maintaining a spotless fellowship with God into which no sin would come. If I did commit sin, I felt, my fellowship with Him would be broken, and He would most certainly withdraw His "blessing" and His approval from me. I would carefully confess my sins, but my life never seemed to improve that much.

I found myself preoccupied with trying not to sin, instead of depending upon Christ to live within me. There was nothing worse than to tell the Lord in the morning that this day would be His and that I wanted my life completely under His control and then to have something go haywire later in the day, culminating in hate thoughts or inner anger and being plagued by a total sense of failure for the rest of the day.

My lack of assurance regarding forgiveness had nothing to do with the things I had done before I was a Christian. I *knew* those were forgiven. The question that arose in my mind again and again was, "What does God do with sins you commit, and even enjoy, after you become His son?"

Answers that came in response to this were varied. They all seemed to have an "if" clause, and the "if" involved would invariably be dependent upon something I must do. Thus, rather than my faith and trust in Jesus Christ increasing, my attention continued to move deeper into my personal spiritual performance.

All this time I was actively relaying the message of Christ to others, especially students, and truly enjoying myself. People were responding to Him with enthusiasm, and in this I found great encouragement.

In order to compensate for the abyss that existed between what I saw in the life of Jesus and what was present in my own experience, I developed an artificial "cosmetic" Christianity. I was subtly moving away from the simple love and trust in Christ with which I had begun, and I tended toward a religious system of performance and duty. When I interacted with people whom I could not love, I learned to speak a vocabulary with inflections that *sounded* like I was concerned. Through sales training in the past, I had learned the importance of eye contact when conversing with others. I developed a way of *looking* like I really cared. Often I did care; other times I did not. People could not tell the difference. With practice, I began to be unaware of this facade myself.

My attitude toward God slipped into a "job-centered" relationship. Instead of depending on Him for my life, I began relying upon Him mainly for the tasks I needed to do. For example, from the middle of my senior year in college until the present, I have been asked to share my Christian experience in group meetings. I would pray and ask God to "re-fill" me with the Holy Spirit and to keep any sin out of my life until the meeting ended. It was like calling up the national guard for an emergency! God, by the way, was always faithful in these times. To me, this vividly demonstrates His matchless and gracious love.

To perform my Christian tasks I *needed* God. I needed His help because I was convinced then, as I am now, that influencing men spiritually must be done through the Holy Spirit and not through the fleshly strength of the human frame.

For me, and I can see it far more clearly now than I ever did in the past, the key issue was my mix-up on total forgiveness. The problem may have stemmed from the beginning of my Christian life when I recognized Jesus more as an example and a standard of life than as my Savior with whom I lived in vital union.

But what happened and what went wrong is not really important to me now. My new life is! And it is this new life which I so eagerly wish to share in the pages that follow.

I am thankful for everything that has occurred both before and after my new understanding of the endless love of God. He has used it all for good. The people whom I have known and with whom I have been associated since becoming a Christian are among the loveliest in God's creation. My experiences with Christ since college have been varied and adventuresome.

But what God has done down inside me — where the human spirit lives — makes me feel like I have been through a spiritual renaissance. God has performed a "happening" for me, and it's still happening. This is no "one day the light dawned" story. God is still unveiling His love and pardon to one who keeps on needing it. It seems I have begun life anew both with Jesus Christ and with my fellow-man.

> "And if the beginning be so sweet,
> What must the end of believing be?"[2]

He hath not dealt with us after our sins; nor rewarded us according to our iniquities. For as the heaven is high above the earth, so great is his mercy toward them that fear him. As far as the east is from the west, so far hath he removed our transgressions from us.

Psalm 103:10-12

2. God Is Absent-Minded

Not long ago I was talking with a neighbor, a typical suburban college grad with a wife, two kids, and nowhere to go but up.

"I've stopped going to church," he said, almost with a sense of pride. "I'm sick and tired of being chewed out every Sunday and always being told I'm wrong. Don't misunderstand — I don't want to be told I'm a good guy either. I just want something definite; I want a way to really *live.*"

He was an easy person with whom to identify. I suggested that he was rejecting a sin-centered message and wanted a forgiveness-centered message instead. With enthusiasm, he agreed.

So much of the typical Christian emphasis today concerns what we *do* rather than what we *are.* The church as a whole has become impotent and listless as a result. Instead of getting back to the essentials of what it is that changes a person, many Christian spokesmen are preaching a works-centered, achievement-based, quasi-Christianity. We hear "get involved," "redouble your efforts," "give more," "sin less," "love your neighbor," "why have you not been more faithful?" until we are numb.

Is not what we are doing with this approach treating the symptoms instead of the causes? God's pattern is that works follow faith, not vice versa.[1] But somehow we have developed the mentality that through constant "challenges," people will be motivated to produce and live Christian lives.

The response this message has produced is varied. Among the older people in society there is perhaps the least response. They are neither for nor against the exhortations to achievement. They are just accustomed to them. Among the young set, wide reaction has occurred. How many "second generation Christians" do you know who are deeply responsive to the things of God? There is, I think, a greater tendency on the part of the high school and college-age crowd to reject the message of performance, but not to seriously look again to God to find an alternative. They search elsewhere.

Between these two groups there is a dissatisfaction with Christianity as it is, but also a deeper probing within the church to come up with some answers. Home discussions, Bible studies, koinonia groups, and similar expressions of renewal are cropping up all across this country.

But regardless of the age group or background, the deadness of the Christian proclamation of today is producing a new concern and a new openness for other avenues of approach. We are looking for a fresh touch from the Spirit of God; for a word which will again ignite a flame of reality and new life within us.

God has spoken such a word. He has been speaking it all along. But it has been lost amid the maze of religious rehash which has blunted the edge of our receptivity to the very life of

Christ itself. It is at the point of His forgiving, person-centered love that we will launch our pilgrimage toward the authentic and compelling life God has promised us.

A NEW SELF-IMAGE

The place God begins in His plan to change our lives is with His forgiveness. The most basic element in the gospel is that in Jesus Christ, God has released us from our sins. Paul said, "For I delivered to you as of first importance what I also received, that Christ died for our sins according to the Scriptures."[2] God says if you have come to Jesus Christ and His kingdom, every sin you have ever committed — past, present, and future — is totally and completely paid for.[3] Even the bad ones. Even the sins that may have hurt others.

We *think* we understand this, but I do not believe we do! There are certain characteristics God says will be evident in the lives of those who are counting on Christ for their forgiveness that simply are not present in the lives of most of us today.

For example, we as believers in Christ possess generally a low image of ourselves. We are down on ourselves, partly because we think God is down on us. We do not see ourselves as forgiven; we see ourselves as not measuring up. We are looking at our actions rather than at Christ. Thus we lack confidence before God. The tendency is to be afraid of Him, rather than to be boldly in love with Him. We see ourselves as having failed.

If we are depending upon Jesus Christ as having cleansed us from our sins, God sees us as perfect. "For by one offering He has perfected for all time those who are sanctified."[4] There is nothing we can do to improve on that which God has declared perfect! And He can say this because through Jesus Christ we have met Him on His terms.

God's ways are so contrary to our ways.[5] We have a hard time understanding His acceptance of us because so much of our orientation in life is achievement-centered. When we were small children, we were told we could have candy *if* we were good. We went to Sunday school and started working for attendance buttons. We joined the scouts and sweated it out for merit badges. In high school, the guys had to make the football team, and the girls tried out for cheerleaders or pom-poms. Senior year came, and some of us took batteries of tests in an attempt to qualify for college. Once we found ourselves in the swirl of campus life, the performance system heightened: Greek life, grades, academic honors, political offices *et alii*. We entered each semester on the basis of how we measured up the semester before, and we had to make it to graduate. If we went right from high school to work, we discovered we were trying to impress a boss who was trying to impress *his* boss.

Is it any wonder that we balk when God comes along and says He'll take us just as we are? After all, we've performed for everything we've gained up to this point; we learned long ago there really is no such thing as free lunch. But God says Jesus Christ has qualified *for* us and now we are perfect in Him.

It does something to you to know someone else thinks you are perfect. It tears down any barriers that might exist. For example, on the person-to-person level, when a man tells his sweetheart she is perfect for him, and she really knows and believes it, her confidence and self-image soar in his presence. She no longer has to be under any pressure at all to prove herself. When a coach tells an athlete he has great ability, his motion becomes all the more fluid. Acceptance by that coach forms a solid base and a certainty from which to operate. And when God says we are perfect in His sight, *we are!* It removes the pressure from us to give Him a snow job with our lives and frees us to live authentically by the power of His Spirit within us.

It is a diluted message which says the cross satisfied God for eternity but not for time. God says we are forgiven *now!* Both

for time and for eternity. You are a new person if you are in Christ. Your sins are forever gone. And it is not just your *acts* which are forgiven; *you* are forgiven.[6] God looks at you as being clean. He has remade the real you. You not only have a new, clean suit of clothes, but the person inside is new, too.

FREEDOM FROM GUILT

Another huge dilemma for the Christian living under today's "gospel" is this matter of guilt. Guilt is based upon the shortcomings of the past. If we could somehow be removed from what went on before, instead of having problems with guilt, we would be resounding with thanksgiving for forgiveness.

Where there is no assurance of forgiveness, there is no true basis for an unthreatened relationship with God. If we are unaware that He has dealt with our past, guilt is bound to result. And the problem is complicated all the more when we read in our Bibles that our lives are to be inwardly and outwardly different — and they're not.

In Hebrews 10, a classic passage on forgiveness, the chapter begins with a summary discussion of the Old Testament sacrificial system and moves quickly into the application of these truths to the person and work of Jesus Christ. We read in verse 2 that had the animal sacrifices really worked, "the worshipers, having once been cleansed, would no longer have had consciousness of sins." The implication is almost too good to be true. The following verse says, "But in those sacrifices there is a reminder of sins year by year."

In other words, God is saying that a reminder of sins is just the opposite from not being conscious of sins. In Jesus Christ we need no longer be plagued with a gloom-cloud awareness of our sins.

We know the Old Testament sacrifice was a picture of the sacrifice of Jesus which was to come. Since the death of Christ on the cross and the sprinkling of His blood on the heavenly mercy seat did satisfy God's demands upon us who were guilty, we can say that His sacrifice "worked." Instead of remembering our sins, as did the Israelites on the Day of Atonement, God wants us to believe they are forgiven, covered, and gone, never to haunt us again.

The sacrifices of old were not God's final plan; they were but a picture of the sacrifice of Jesus on the cross which *was* God's final plan of forgiveness. Hebrews 10:12 says, "He, having offered *one* sacrifice for sins for *all time*, sat down at the right hand of God" (italics mine). And since His payment was more than sufficient, we need no longer have a consciousness of sin!

Hebrews 10:17 explains why this is true. God says, "And their sins and their lawless deeds I will remember no more." When it comes to our sins, God has forgotten them. He has buried them in the deepest seas.[7] He has separated them as far from us as the East is from the West.[8] They are hidden in the clouds.[9] When it comes to remembering our sins, God is absent-minded!

Guilt is such a screaming thing; forgiveness is so quiet. We often pay more attention to the noise of accusation than to the silence of sins forgiven. Guilt does not come from God. It originates from the lingering accusations of Satan. And we tend to turn our attention to the accuser who condemns rather than to Christ who forgives.

I talk with people who say, "I committed a sin, and I know God has forgiven me, but I still feel guilty." Well, all right, it's a *feeling*. But what is more dependable, the promises of Jesus Christ or the way we feel? Psychologists tell us feelings are extremely undependable and sometimes even unpredictable. Some mornings I get up and feel no more like a Christian than a jack rabbit! It is *so* important to trust in Jesus Christ rather than in how we feel.

In the early days of aviation, pilots used a descriptive little phrase, "Flying by the seat of your pants." Before instruments were widely available on planes as they are today, the only guide for air navigation in inclement weather was by means of physical sensation. If you felt pressure upon the seat of the aircraft, it probably meant you were ascending, much the same as the feeling you get in a rising elevator. Conversely, if there was a sensation of weightlessness, it most likely meant the plane was on the descent. This means of flying was not at all reliable. Men met their deaths because their feelings played tricks on them.

God has not left us to operate simply on the basis of human emotion. When He says we are forgiven, He means it, whether we always feel forgiven or not. And He has sent the Holy Spirit to live in our hearts to personally authenticate His promise to us.

While on the Notre Dame campus a few years ago, I met a student who had discovered the truth that God forgives and forgets. He used the illustration of a person who had sinned and admitted it to the Lord. Ten minutes later he committed the same sin and muttered, "Oh, God, there I went and did it again." A big booming voice came out of the clouds and said, "Did what?"

That's crude but vivid. God really does willingly forget our sins. He so totally placed them upon His Son that when Jesus died, He took *all* of our sins with Him to the grave. Had He missed one of them, we would be hopeless. James said, "For whoever keeps the whole law and yet stumbles in one point, he has become guilty of all."[10] Jesus had to bear every sin in all the world for the sacrifice to be effectual. And if you have trusted in Him, every sin that you have ever committed or ever will commit is *totally* and *completely* forgiven.

I somehow thought, even as a Christian, that when I died and went to be with God, He would drag out a huge, long list of all my offenses and read it off to me. I assumed I would begin eternity with a deficit balance. God's plan, in antithesis to all of this, is that Jesus paid off my debt and no such list exists. In fact, this is one of the greatest things about becoming a Christian. God not only wipes the slate clean, He also throws the slate away. We pass from death into life. "There is therefore now no condemnation for those who are in Christ Jesus."[11] We are released from our sins.

The question may come to mind. "If God forgets all my sins, what on earth is it about me that He remembers?"

"For God is not unjust so as to forget your work and the love which you have shown toward His name, in having ministered and in still ministering to the saints."[12]

What is it that God recalls about you and me for all eternity? Our good works. The things we do in response to His living Word — our obedience as we hear from Him. Thus, our identity with God is no longer one of condemnation, but one of commendation. He has forgotten our evil deeds of sin and rebellion and sees us as clothed in the righteousness of Jesus Christ for our walk together in the Holy Spirit.

A NEW AWARENESS OF ACCEPTANCE

Now here's the exciting thing: if God has forgotten my sins, I can forget them too. The barrier does not exist between God and me any more. That's what it means to no longer have a consciousness of sin: to see our sins as God sees them — judged, paid for, buried, and gone.

So often our attention is focused on our sin and its badness, rather than on Christ and His goodness. We live, in effect, sin-centered lives instead of Christ-centered lives. Somehow we become convinced that holiness involves trying not to sin. God, on the other hand, frees us to forget our sins and depend upon Jesus Christ for our righteousness.

Suppose I get out of bed in the morning and think to myself, "All right, your three biggest sins are temper, lust, and criticism of other people. Today, I will not become angry, I will not lust, and I will not criticize others. And, God, I want You to help me." By setting up a list of "don'ts," I am already indulging in them.

It's like going on a diet and making a mental list of the twelve things you can't eat. You read in your Bible that your body is the temple of the Holy Spirit, and you plainly do not want a fat temple! So with your list of prohibitions in mind, you walk through the cafeteria line. And guess what you crave more than anything else — that which you cannot have. Trying not to sin makes us sin more. God says forget it. What a difference! In essence, my attitude toward sin can be: "Thank You, Lord, that I'm totally and completely forgiven for all my sins. Instead of trying not to sin today, I'm just going to trust You. Thanks for setting me free, Father, to receive the righteousness You are producing within me."

Put this book down for a moment and picture in your mind a red-faced monkey. Got it? Now, the moment you finish reading this sentence, erase from your mind the image of the red-faced monkey. Doesn't work, does it? I am alarmed when I think of how we do the same thing with sin! Instead of believing that sin is covered through the blood of Christ, we resurrect it from the dead. God is satisfied by the Lord Jesus, and we can add nothing on our own to increase His satisfaction.

It is interesting that the apostle Peter picks up this same truth in his second letter. As he begins the book, the thesis of his first chapter is growth in the Christian life. He starts out by reminding his readers that all things have been given to them pertaining to life and godliness. Then he admonishes them to add to their faith moral excellence, knowledge, self-control, perseverance, godliness, brotherly kindness, and finally godly love. He says if these qualities are in their lives and are on the increase, they will be fruitful in their walk with God. He then tells them why they aren't growing as they ought: "For he who lacks these qualities is blind or shortsighted, having forgotten his purification from his former sins."[13]

What is God's analysis of the problem of stunted spiritual growth and development? It's clearly not our failure to go to church, have devotions, think clean thoughts, and all our other Christian solutions. Our problem is *we've forgotten we're forgiven.* We've failed to remember Jesus was not kidding when He said, "Your sins have been forgiven."[14]

When we are trusting Jesus Christ, life — His life within us — is the beautiful by-product. What is more real to you right now: your failures so far this day or Jesus Christ? If it's the former, don't worry; you're forgiven! The solution for the failure? Faith. Trust. Counting on Him. *He* sees *you* as a restored human being, possessing the very life of God on high.

It does not depend on the man who wills or the man who runs, but on God who has mercy.

Romans 9:16

3. Portraits of Forgiveness

When our first child, Wendy Jo, was four years old, God taught us a beautiful lesson through her. It was after dinner, and her mother had just put her to bed. At that time, we lived in a rather small, two-bedroom apartment. Often Marilyn would put Wendy to bed in our bedroom and the other children in the nursery, to help keep them from talking with each other while they were supposed to be asleep.

Marilyn was out in the kitchen finishing the dishes when she heard Wendy jumping on our bed. She walked back to our bedroom and told her to quiet down. A few minutes later, the jumping resumed. This time the instruction was much more specific. "If I have to tell you again," Marilyn told Wendy, "you will get a spanking. Besides, mommy's favorite lamp is on the table next to the bed, and I'd feel terrible if anything were to happen to it. Now be quiet and go to sleep."

The lamp on our bedside table was one of the prettiest we had ever seen and was just right for the room. It had come from a large, stately home on the North Shore in the beautiful Chicago suburb of Winnetka. We were always sure to have it aglow when guests came to call.

Back in the kitchen for the third time, Marilyn thought she heard the sound of a bouncing child. Just before she reached the bedroom there was a distinct crash.

After the execution of the spanking, Marilyn took Wendy in her arms, hugged her, and said, "I spanked you because you bounced on the bed after I told you not to." Marilyn then proceeded to sweep up the remains of the shattered lamp. Wendy watched with dismay. When all the pieces were removed from the floor and the lamp was solemnly discarded in the trash box, Marilyn told her, "As far as the lamp is concerned, mommy loves you and forgives you, and I'll never mention it to you again."

The next day Marilyn was walking through the apartment and inadvertently stepped on one of Wendy's toys and smashed it. She felt terrible. Wendy ran over and picked it up and said, "Mommy, I forgive you for that, and I'll never ever mention it to you again."

What a portrait of forgiveness! When we really grasp it, our lives are changed without self-effort. That is why forgiveness is a proof of God's love. [1] We know we are loved because we know we are forgiven. God wants us to see ourselves as totally forgiven, just the way He sees us. His forgiveness affects not only our understanding of His love for us, but it affects the love we show for ourselves, for others (as was the case with Wendy Jo), and for God Himself. *Our view of forgiveness really determines our love for God.*

Jesus had been invited to dine with a Pharisee named Simon. [2] During the meal, the intimate party was interrupted by a woman of the street, a prostitute. For no apparent reason, she walked up to the Lord and, weeping, began to wet His feet with her tears. Then she wiped them with her hair, kissed them, and anointed them with perfume. Simon the Pharisee was angry. His plans for the evening were in jeopardy.

"This woman is ruining my dinner party," he no doubt thought to himself. "Here's my chance to make some points with the Lord, and she is ruining the whole affair. Besides, if Jesus were that much of a prophet, He'd spot her for what she is, a real loser."

Just then Jesus spoke up. Let's join the biblical text:

> "Simon, I have something to say to you." And he replied, "Say it, Teacher." "A certain money-lender had two debtors: one owed him five hundred denarii, and the other fifty. When they were unable to repay, he graciously forgave them both. Which of them therefore will love him more?"[3]

Now Simon was probably shrewd when it came to business deals. It was no secret to anyone that he had some denarii signs in his eyes. Jesus was speaking his language. Simon caught the point and came up with the right answer. "The one who got off the hook for the greater amount," he said.

It is here the grace of the Lord Jesus Christ really comes through. Here was Simon who, as a Pharisee, knew all the right answers, but he didn't know the right questions. The woman, on the other hand, had some questions, but was short on answers. In fact she was low on questions too. But she knew that Jesus had a quality of life that was foreign to her own experience. Instead of asking Him questions, she simply showed up at the dinner and tried to convey her feelings for Him as best she could. The biblical text does not record one word she said. Jesus knows men's hearts. "Man looketh on the outward appearance, but the Lord looketh on the heart."[4] The desire of her heart toward Him was far greater than that of Simon. Jesus took her as she was.

> And turning toward the woman, He said to Simon, "Do you see this woman? I entered your house; you gave Me no water for My feet, but she has wet My feet with her tears, and wiped them with her hair. You gave Me no kiss; but she, since the time I came in, has not ceased to kiss My feet. You did not anoint My head with oil, but she anointed My feet with perfume."[5]

Here were three major customs of the day: the washing of feet, the kiss of greeting, and the anointing of the head with oil. Instead of washing His feet, she cried on them; instead of giving Him the kiss of greeting in the customary fashion on the cheek, she kissed His feet; and instead of anointing His head with oil, she poured perfume on His feet. And the Book of Proverbs suggests that perfume in those days was a mark of the trade of a prostitute.[6] She did everything wrong, but she tried her best to show she loved Him. She somehow must have had the assurance that here was One who could help meet her deepest needs.

Jesus, still addressing Himself to Simon, said, "For this reason I say to you, her sins, which are many, have been forgiven, for she loved much, but he who is forgiven little, loves little."[7]

If we know we are totally forgiven, loving God will come as a direct result. If we, on the other hand, see God as having only partly forgiven our sins, we'll have a tough time loving Him. Our attention will be back on our sins rather than upon Christ and His forgiveness. And the conclusion we will inevitably draw is that God is pleased by our not sinning rather than by Jesus' sacrifice for us.

This was, in essence, Simon's problem. A program of good works to gain God's favor, not faith, was the result. This is not to say God condones sin. But it is to say He desires us to agree with Him that we are forgiven, that Christ is presenting us faultless before Him, so our eyes will be taken off our sins and turned toward Him. Holiness comes neither by trying to be good nor by trying not to be bad. It comes through depending upon what God says we already are in Jesus Christ and through relying upon Him to remake us into His image through the Holy Spirit.

I had just finished speaking to an exciting group of college students in a fraternity living room at the University of Iowa when a girl came up and said she wanted to talk. "I really like what you said tonight about forgiveness," she said, "but I just can't seem to get it in terms of my experience. I know when I sin, and I know I'm wrong when I do it, but I still keep right on living in my rut."

We sat down and began to talk, and I inquired about her background. "When did you come to know Christ?" I asked.

"It was when I was nine," she responded. "I was baptized at that time. But I still don't understand what it means to be forgiven. You say that when you really count on your forgiveness, you find life changing, and I'm not seeing mine changed at all."

During the next twenty minutes or so, we went through every major passage with which I was familiar in the New Testament on the subject of forgiveness. We talked about the fact that God sees us as perfect in Christ and that He not only forgives, but also forgets our sins. We discussed the importance of remembering our forgiveness if we do sin. Still the haze refused to lift. She just did not get the picture. In fact, it was as though we were conversing about two entirely different subjects, she one and I another.

Finally, I said, "If you promise not to get angry, I'll tell you what I think your problem is."

"What's that?" she asked.

"You're not really a Christian," I replied, expecting the worst.

"I was afraid of that," she admitted. "Christ never has been real to me."

We prayed together, and with gratefulness she invited Jesus to enter her heart and life. She thanked Him for cleansing her from everything in her past, her present, her future. After we finished praying, we talked for a few minutes more. Then, spying a friend across the room, she rushed over to tell her what had happened — that she now had a personal relationship with Jesus Christ. On her way out the door, she turned to say good-by. Her last words before she left were, "I *know* that I'm forgiven."

Forgiveness is the starting point of our faith. I am convinced if more people knew from the initial moments of their life with Christ that their sins were no longer an issue, we would see far fewer problems in Christians' lives. Man needs to know he can be made new! Medical reports tell us that something like 50 percent of the hospital beds in this country are filled with mental patients,[8] and many of them are suffering from guilt. What a tragedy that even many of us who say we know Christ are all up tight over our sins, when we should be standing tall in our forgiveness, letting God remake us as we walk in obedience with Him.

One of the things that has helped me to see more clearly the complete forgiveness in the blood of Jesus Christ is to understand more fully the historical pattern from which it was taken. On the Day of Atonement in the Old Testament, forgiveness is portrayed with prophetic clarity. The record and its applications are found in Hebrews 9.

The tabernacle of Israel was constructed with two rooms in tandem. The two chambers were separated by a veil. The outer part was called the Holy Place. It was into this section that the priest entered regularly to make the daily sacrifices to God.

But the inner tabernacle, the Holy of Holies, was visited only one day each year by the high priest on the Day of Atonement. The Holy of Holies was permeated with the glory of God.

Inside this second chamber was the ark of the covenant containing three objects: (1) a golden jar of manna; (2) Aaron's rod which budded; and (3) the tablets of the law. It can be said that these three items embodied in a symbolic way the sins of mankind. The manna was a picture of man's rejection of God's provisions for him. The rod of Aaron symbolized man's rejection of God's leadership. The tablets of the law illustrated man's rejection of the holiness of God. Across the top of the ark the priest could see what was called the mercy seat, or the place of grace.

Overlooking the mercy seat were two angel-like figures called cherubim, representing the holy character of God. One stood for the justice of God, which says, in effect, "The soul that sinneth, it shall die,"[9] or, "The wages of sin is death."[10] The other cherubim signified the righteousness of God, which says, "Be ye holy; for I am holy."[11] God does not grade on the curve; His standards are absolute! This whole scene was a picture of God looking down upon man and seeing there was no hope at all for man through his efforts to enter His presence. Because of God's righteousness and man's sinfulness, fellowship was hopeless — apart from the forgiveness and presence of God.

Once each year on the Day of Atonement, the high priest, having entered the Holy of Holies, would sprinkle the blood of a spotless animal substitute upon the mercy seat. During what amounted to 364 days of the year (using the Gregorian year for reasons of simplicity), the cherubim gazed down upon the sins of man and saw him guilty. On this 365th day the same cherubim would look down upon the same ark, but this day sin was *covered*, covered by the blood of an innocent replacement. The justice of God would see in the blood the death penalty as having already been paid and would be satisfied with the sacrifice. The righteousness of God looked down to see that it was righteous blood and, therefore, saw righteousness instead of sin. Thus, the portrait of the blood sacrifice.

This happened just one day out of the year. But the Hebrews standing outside the tabernacle during this event on the Day of Atonement were fully cognizant of its consequences. As long as that high priest was inside the Holy of Holies, their sins were being covered by the blood of a spotless animal. God saw their sins as covered and so did they.

But here's the important thing to understand. Those Hebrews knew that while the high priest was in the inner chamber as their representative in His presence, there was *fellowship with God.* If Christ is our great High Priest and is in the presence of God right this moment in our behalf, presenting us as perfect before the throne,[12] what does that say about the basis of our fellowship with the Father? Upon what does our fellowship with God depend — the things we do for Him or the things He does for us?

Because Christ has come before the holy throne of God for us, if we are trusting in Him and in the authenticity of His sacrifice for us, we are in complete, unbroken, intimate fellowship with the eternal God! There is no way to upgrade a relationship like that. We did nothing to deserve it, nothing to bring it about, and it is certain we can do nothing to maintain it. That fellowship with our lovely God has been and is being and will be accomplished completely for us by His Son, our personal representative, Jesus Christ. The veil is now gone.

I make a special issue of this point because some believers are caught in an "in and out of fellowship" trap. They are so preoccupied with trying to blow out their sins and breathe in forgiveness to maintain fellowship with God that they are left gasping for air! This matter of fellowship with God will be dealt with more fully in the next chapter. But, at this point, remember — *Christ* has won your fellowship with God.

For the Israelite, his "once-a-year day" was both glad and sad. It was glad because all his sins of the past year were covered and declared gone. It was sad because a new scorecard for the ensuing year was put into effect. It would be another year before he could experience again this cleansing of the flesh.

I was speaking at a retreat to a group of students from several midwestern universities. My topic that particular Saturday afternoon was the Atonement and its foundations in the Old Testament. During my talk, I said, "We as believers in Jesus Christ sometimes take for granted our forgiveness in Him. Can you imagine anything worse than being forgiven only one day a year?" A student in the back of the room, who had just prayed with me the night before to receive Christ, quipped, "Yeah, never having been forgiven at all!"

The Old Testament sacrificial system was the best thing going at the time. I'm sure when we go to be with God we shall meet Old Testament believers by the droves. But as wonderful as that heritage is, it is but a shadow when compared to the permanence and the incomprehensible depth of the riches of freedom from sin in the Lamb which God provided,[13] the Lord Jesus. We can echo the words of Micah: "Who is a God like unto thee, that pardoneth iniquity, and passeth by the transgression of the remnant of his heritage? he retaineth not his anger for ever, because he delighteth in mercy."[14]

I will bear the indignation of the Lord, be-
cause I have sinned against him, until he plead
my cause, and execute judgment for me: he
will bring me forth to the light, and I shall
behold his righteousness.   Micah 7:9

4.   An Obsession
With Confession

Perhaps by this point the question has arisen in your mind,
"Well, if my sins were totally forgiven by the blood of Christ
— if God really has forgotten them as He says He has — why
does the Scripture also tell us to confess our sins?" What is the
meaning of 1 John 1:9 when it exhorts, "If we confess our sins,
He is faithful and righteous to forgive us our sins and to cleanse
us from all unrighteousness"?

The whole matter of once-for-all forgiveness versus confession arose in my mind shortly after I came to know Christ. I can
remember one night in particular when a friend and I struggled
with the issue into the early hours of the morning. I had gone
east to meet Gordon Walker, who at that time was living in
Xenia, Ohio. We started to bat the issue around after returning
to our room one night. Admitting that there was no apparent

answer to the dilemma, the last thing we agreed upon before falling asleep was, "This must be one of those seeming contradictions which will be answered when we get to heaven."

For years it appeared to me that when we received Christ, all our sins were forgiven and forgotten only up to the point of conversion. This was what total forgiveness meant. From that point on, however, the way we stayed cleansed was by confession to God on each item of sin. And I wasn't against confessing my sins, for the Scriptures teach confession.

My problem was twofold: (1) keeping that "short account" with God — making sure I was always "'fessed up" (which had me operating as my own, personal Holy Spirit!); and (2) making sure I caught *all* my sins in order to acknowledge them, which meant if I had missed something, I'd be out of fellowship with the Lord. (Any sins I didn't know about, I conveniently thought, would be "automatically" forgiven.)

I would meet other Christians for whom sins did not seem to pose that much of a problem. They rarely discussed the matter. Their conversation revolved around Jesus Christ and the joy that comes from Him. Sin did not seem to enter into their relationship and spoil it. Or I would read the Scriptures and *never* notice Paul, Peter, Titus, Timothy, or John complaining that they had problems with getting out of fellowship with God. This business of being in and out of fellowship all the time *just wasn't taught!*

One afternoon, another friend, Jon Braun, and I became engrossed in a conversation on the same topic that Gordon Walker and I had mulled over three years earlier. As we were talking in our living room, Jon remarked, "The other day I was in the library taking notes on what I was reading, and 1 John 1:7 said something to me that I had never been aware of before. If it says what I think it says, we need to change the thrust of what we've been teaching."

We turned to the passage, and I read silently: "But if we walk in the light as He Himself is in the light, we have fellowship with one another, and the blood of Jesus His Son cleanses us from all sin."

"According to that passage, where are you walking when you commit the sin?" he asked. It took me a few moments to see it, because I had never considered a question like that at all. "In the light," I said with great amazement.

"That's the point," Jon said. "The blood of Christ keeps us clean as we walk with Him in the light. We don't slip back into the darkness each time we sin. Rather, if we are walking in the light and *do* commit a sin, it is His blood that keeps us clean."

For the first time, the burden of trying to *stay* forgiven began to lift. And let me say clearly: there is nothing wrong with agreeing with God when you sin. In fact, the natural response of a cleansed, forgiven heart is to agree. *But we are not cleansed from sin by confession, and we never have been!* Not even under the Old Covenant were people cleansed by confession. Forgiveness always has come and always will come through the blood sacrifice for sin. *We are forgiven today by the blood of Jesus Christ.*

The thing that excited me was realizing that if Jesus Christ would *keep* me clean, there was no reason why I ever had to be out of fellowship with God again. But what did it mean to be in fellowship, in the light? Where did confession of sin come into the picture? I still did not see how it all fit together.

WHAT IS THE BACKGROUND OF 1 JOHN?

Two years and scores of hours of study and interaction centered around the book of 1 John have followed. I am enamored by its priceless and simple message of life in Christ. I have discovered it is far more than just "one of those short books near the end of the Bible." Its message sets us free from the bondage and depression of sin!

The apostle John wrote his first epistle at the end of the first century, in about A.D. 90, partly to help combat an error called "gnosticism" that had crept into the early church. The Gnostics taught that Jesus was not really human. They said He could not be in bodily form and still be God. In line with this, they also denied His preexistence and taught that the Father created Him at a point in time. Closely aligned with this error was the Gnostic denial, in a practical sense, of the reality of sin. They maintained the old Greek view of the inherent evil in matter. Thus, that which is material or physical is naturally bad, and that which is nonmaterial or spiritual is naturally good. This not only capsized their view of sin, but it also meant that the person of Christ was split into a hopeless dichotomy — the spiritual part of Jesus, which was good, and the material part of Jesus, which was bad.[1]

With this brief background, it is clear why John, in writing his first epistle, began in the manner in which he did.

> 1:1. What was from the beginning, what we have heard, what we have seen with our eyes, what we beheld, and our hands handled, concerning the Word of life —
>
> 1:2. and the life was manifested, and we have seen and bear witness and proclaim to you the eternal life, which was with the Father and was manifested to us —
>
> 1:3. what we have seen and heard we proclaim to you also, that you also may have fellowship with us; and indeed our fellowship is with the Father, and with His Son Jesus Christ.

As you read over the above statement describing the life which Jesus presents to us, you will notice John's allusions to the Gnostic problem. He covers the fact that Jesus has existed forever, that He was physically observable, and that He is viewed as a totally constituted person — 100 percent Son of man and 100 percent Son of God. In the opening sentence of this letter, John is laying the foundation of the reality of the incarnation of the Lord Jesus Christ: that God the Son took on full humanity, being born into the world as a real, knowable person, fully God and fully man.

Starting in verse 5 John compares the way true Christians believe and behave with the excuses and life styles of those in error. John is the author of contrasts. In fact, the comparison-contrast method of pedagogy was inherent within the whole tradition of the Jewish heritage, of which the apostle was a part. Often the best way to understand a concept is to see it contrasted with something else. And this is the tool John employs in 1 John to help his readers understand. The key to interpreting these early verses is not to see *that* he is comparing and contrasting, but to see *what* he is comparing and contrasting. When we see his contrast, we get a valuable understanding of God's forgiveness.

In 1 John 1:5-10, John begins contrasting two specific kinds of people. To make the distinction live, he employs two words — *darkness* and *light* — used also in other parts of the New Testament as synonyms for his two categories. Here is what he says:

1:5. And this is the message which we have heard from Him and announce to you, that God is light, and in Him there is no darkness at all.

1:6. If we say that we have fellowship with Him and yet walk in the darkness, we lie and do not practice the truth;

1:7. but if we walk in the light as He Himself is in the light, we have fellowship with one another, and the blood of Jesus His Son cleanses us from all sin.

1:8. If we say that we have no sin, we are deceiving ourselves, and the truth is not in us.

1:9. If we confess our sins, He is faithful and righteous to forgive us our sins and to cleanse us from all unrighteousness.

1:10. If we say that we have not sinned, we make Him a liar, and His word is not in us.

LIGHT AND DARKNESS

The two key words in this particular section of the book, *darkness* and *light*, help characterize the two groups being contrasted and lead to John's usage of the word *confess*. Let's stop here for a moment and look briefly at several other New Testament passages which help us clearly ascertain the meaning of light and darkness.

In Acts 26:18 we have a significant usage of these two words. Paul is quoting from what Jesus said to him during his encounter with Christ on the road to Damascus. Luke records it as follows: "to open their eyes so that they may turn from darkness to light and from the dominion of Satan to God, in order that they may receive forgiveness of sins and an inheritance among those who have been sanctified by faith in Me." Notice that Jesus tells Paul his role in life will be to help turn the Gentiles from one kingdom or dominion to another, that is, from the domain of Satan to the kingdom of God. Darkness is synonymous with Satan's dominion, and light describes the kingdom of God. In God's kingdom there is forgiveness of sins and the promise of an inheritance.

Closely related in content with this Acts passage is 1 Thessalonians 5:1-6. In these verses Paul is beginning his answer to a question posed by the Thessalonian church regarding the day of the Lord and when it will take place. He starts out by assuring them that even though Christ will come without notice, the suddenness of that day will bring no fear for believers, because "you, brethren, are not in darkness, that the day should overtake you like a thief; for you are all sons of light and sons of day. We are not of night nor of darkness." In this passage the thrust of the Acts 26 impact is enhanced. We see that *all* true believers are sons of the light. Christians have no part in the darkness.

In Colossians 1:12-13, another important reference is made

to light and darkness. It is interesting to note that the Book of Colossians was also written to help combat the problem of gnosticism. Here Paul is "giving thanks to the Father, who has qualified us to share in the inheritance of the saints in light. For He delivered us from the domain of darkness, and transferred us to the kingdom of His beloved Son." It is God through what He does, and not we through what we do, who makes us qualified to be with the saints in light. In pro golf, a tournament entrant needs to shoot a qualifying round before he can ever enter the final rounds for the prize money. In the Christian life, God shoots the qualifying round for us! In verse 13 both the words *delivered* and *transferred* are in definite past action construction. A parallel passage states: "For you were formerly darkness but now you are light in the Lord."[2] Our deliverance and transfer from darkness to light are absolutely accomplished.

Taking this information back into the First Epistle of John, it is fully apparent the two groups in contrast here are believers and unbelievers; he is talking about those who are in the light and walking in the light, and those who are in the darkness and walking in the darkness.

In fact, here's an interesting line-up of individual verses in 1 John 1 and 2 that makes this distinction even more apparent. Read through these verses and ask yourself whether they are describing believers or unbelievers:

> 1:6   If we say that we have fellowship with Him and yet walk in the darkness, we lie and do not practice the truth;
>
> 1:8   If we say that we have no sin, we are deceiving ourselves, and the truth is not in us.
>
> 1:10 If we say that we have not sinned, we make Him a liar, and His word is not in us.
>
> 2:4   The one who says, "I have come to know Him," and does not keep His commandments, is a liar, and the truth is not in him;

2:9   The one who says he is in the light and yet hates his
      brother is in the darkness until now.
2:11 But the one who hates his brother is in the darkness
      and walks in the darkness, and does not know where
      he is going because the darkness has blinded his
      eyes.

THE ISSUE: DO YOU OR DON'T YOU BELIEVE?

To say these passages refer merely to Christians who are out of
fellowship with the Lord seems to me to be a denial of every
other section of Scripture defining the character and quality of
life of a true believer in Jesus Christ. Instead, I believe these
verses refer to unregenerate people, most likely Gnostic in
persuasion.

In 1 John 1:5-10, the apostle answers the threefold ("if we
say") false allegations of gnosticism in verses 6, 8, and 10 by
setting forth the truth in verses 7 and 9. *If we say* we know God
and are still in darkness, we are liars (verse 6). *If we say* we are
not by nature sinful, we are deceived (verse 8). *If we say* we no
longer commit acts of sin, we are saying to God, "You are a
liar!" (verse 10).

By contrast, look at John's rebuttal to these three heretical
slogans. *If we walk* in the light of God, we really *do* know Him
and commune with Him — and, besides, the blood of Jesus
Christ keeps on cleansing us from sin (verse 7). *If we confess*
(literally: if we keep on agreeing with God concerning) our sins,
He, in His trustworthiness and justice, forgives and completely cleanses us (verse 9).

Do you see the simplicity of John's reasoning? The false
brethren *alibied*, the believers *acted*. It's the old story of the
say-ers and the do-ers. They talk, we walk; they profess, we
confess.

For some reason, a small segment of modern Protestants has
taken this section of Scripture and constructed a novel system
whereby believers bounce in and out of fellowship with God.

That is not what the passage teaches. Furthermore, this school of thought has built its system essentially on one Bible verse — 1 John 1:9. It's a great verse, but you don't built a theology on it any more than you build a theology on any other single, isolated verse. (The older I get, the more suspicious I become of shortcut, technique-oriented theology. In the long run, it will not carry you. It's time the church gets back to the foundation of the whole counsel of God and jump down from the crumbly footings of a few theme-song Bible verses!)

As a result, there are people today who say the secret to maintaining fellowship with God is confessing sin. *No it isn't!* Confession is not and never has been a work to attain a mental state of private fellowship with God. Our relationship with God is through our Lord Jesus Christ. If we need a "secret" for fellowship with the Father, it is the Son! The idea of teaching Christians they can be in and out of fellowship with God several times a day is a doctrine not found in the Scriptures. If you persist in holding to it, it will bring you into bondage. Get back to the solid, basic faith. Confessing our sins is as important as one of the evidences that we are in fellowship with the Lord; *it is not a method we practice to stay in.*

GETTING IN FELLOWSHIP — AND STAYING THERE

Way back in Ezekiel 36:26-27, God made an eternal agreement with all who would wish to know Him and be numbered among His people. He told us, "I will give you a new heart and put a new spirit within you; and I will remove the heart of stone from your flesh and give you a heart of flesh. And I will put My Spirit within you and cause you to walk in My statutes."

This promise is also recorded in Jeremiah 31:31-34 and is echoed in Hebrews 8:8-12. It is called the New Covenant. It guarantees that if we are born into God's forever family through Jesus Christ, we will be given new, soft hearts and the Holy Spirit will live within us. He will *cause* us to do God's will. Whereas once our hearts were hardened toward God, now they are pliable and obedient. Whereas once we stood against the Lord, now we have come to stand with Him and agree with Him. Whereas once we walked away from Him, now we are walking with Him in the fullness of His grace and mercy.

This is the contrast John is talking about as he opens his letter. Those in error *say* they have fellowship with God, but we who believe *are* in fellowship, in the light. False brethren *deny* their sins; we *confess* ours. And we keep on walking and keep on agreeing because we know Him and walk in fellowship with Him.

And here the question always seems to come, "But what if a person doesn't confess — is sin still forgiven?" Or, "Is there really such a thing, then, as being out of fellowship?"

Yes, Virginia, there really is an out-of-fellowship! Let me name some names — names the Scriptures name — people in the New Testament who were out of fellowship with God on this earth.

The man in 1 Corinthians 5:1-6. Here was a man in the church at Corinth who was practicing incest. In short, he got the boot; he was put out of fellowship. In verse 5 Paul writes, "I have decided to deliver such a one to Satan for the destruction of his flesh."

Demas. Demas was a co-worker of Paul, having been on hand during those three incomparable years in Ephesus. He witnessed the miracles of God and sat under the best teaching heaven had to offer. But Demas was a deserter. Paul later wrote and told Timothy (2 Tim. 4:10) that Demas had departed from serving God, "having loved this present world."

Hymenaeus and Alexander. Here were two believers whose hearts turned against God, and they blasphemed the Lord. First Timothy 1:19-20 records their spiritual shipwreck.

Early in the history of the church, a term came into being to describe the action taken toward those who had chosen to walk in rebellion against the Lord and His people and who refused, after repeated encouragement, to repent: *excommunication.* Their lack of a repentant attitude was seen, and they were *put* out of fellowship, the same as in 1 Corinthians 5:1-6.

This biblical out-of-fellowshipness is almost a forgotten practice in the church today. In liberal Protestantism, it's gone. In conservative churches when a member falls into repeated sin, he is sometimes snubbed and "prayed for," but seldom really confronted and given the opportunity to turn from the sin or be ejected. Rome has, for the most part, operated under static dogmas, with the voice of the living God in such matters neglected and forgotten. Love still speaks the truth and stands for righteousness. Church, let's get it back.

Along this same line, much of modern Christendom has left repentance out of its message. We don't call on people to *change their minds* concerning sin. Show me a person who has trouble with persistent sin, and I'll most likely show you a person who never turned from it in the first place! Fellow-Christian, the Lord Jesus Christ died to release you from your sins. Turn from them. They're wrong. If you refuse, all the confession in the world won't help. The problem is with your *will*. Church, let's confront this person.

Because of our massive loss of community and authority in the church, we have slipped into our individualistic Christianity. Instead of experiencing true fellowship with God and authoritative discipline in the church, now *I* decide these things for myself. I become my own judge as to what fellowship with God really is and if, in fact, I am in or out of it. Thus, being in fellowship with God no longer has anything to do with our relationship to the church of Jesus Christ. And that sort of individualistic-only fellowship is bogus. It is unheard of in both the New Testament and in historic Christian doctrine.

What a joy to be free from the knots of meaningless confession and to be living in the fellowship God offers under the Lordship of Christ in His church. I honestly have been liberated from the question: Am I in or out of fellowship with God? When you walk with the Lord in the context of His body and commit a sin, should the Holy Spirit have trouble getting through to you about it, He'll certainly send by some of the brethren to give you a "body-check." There is authority in the church of Jesus Christ, and it is good to be a man under such authority.

Do I confess sin? Of course I do. With a new heart and a new Spirit, the agreement that I am sinful is there. And the love of God is so great that even when I forget to agree, there is a Savior who died for my forgetfulness, too. Which must explain why the old revivalists kept on telling their hearers, "You can't out-sin the grace of God!" Their open reverence for God's holy mercy steered their hearers away from license and into vital righteousness.

God's love for us provides an environment of relationship that is without threat. I have spiritual life within me which engenders trust in Him. Knowing that my union with Christ is based with permanence upon His love for me not only produces a new breed of honesty and openness with Him if I do disobey, but also motivates me to really want to do what He says. There is no fear in love.[3] And my attentiveness is turned from its introspective focus on sin to a new and fresh perception of Jesus Christ. As a result, I have a different attitude and deeper personal relationship.

Unconditional love on the part of God, and in our own experience, does not mean we soft-pedal the matter of sin. Love forgives sin, but it does not endorse it. God, in His love, paid an infinite price to forgive us. He did not assume the attitude that boys will be boys and sweep the matter under the rug. Love *gives*. And God gave His only Son to forgive us and release us from our sins. The cost to Him was great.

A CLEAN BREAK

One more thing — God not only *forgives* us, with no strings attached, but He also *keeps* us clean. Earlier in this chapter I spoke of 1 John 1:7, which literally says He "constantly keeps on continually cleansing us from sin."

Have you ever had the problem of thinking something evil and then attempting to get rid of it? You say, "Lord, forgive me," and it pops right back into your mind again. So you ask Him to forgive the second thought, and still no results. You don't want to do it. I've been that thought-poppin' route so often I'm sick of it.

As I was driving one day from Toledo to Ann Arbor, I began feasting on a bad thought. The Lord reminded me that since I was walking in the light as He is in the light and was having fellowship with Him, His blood was constantly, completely cleansing me from my sin. What a fantastic truth. It is not up to me to get forgiven, but up to Him to forgive — and He has already done it! As I simply *believed* Him (agreed with Him, confessed), the thought left. As a matter of fact, I don't even remember what it was.

We are forgiven. Why make an effort to get out from under sin when Jesus says it's already gone?

With these things in mind, 1 John 2:1-2 come alive. "My little children, I am writing these things to you that you may not sin. And if anyone sins, we have an Advocate with the Father, Jesus Christ the righteous; and He Himself is the propitiation for our sins; and not for ours only, but also for those of the whole world."

The author directs his letter to the believers, the "little children," and says that in view of what he has written in the first chapter, we no longer *have* to sin. Knowing we are forgiven, knowing that Christ is our life, sin is no longer inevitable. It goes back to this thing of not having a consciousness of sin. God wants us to be conscious of our Savior, not of our sins. He wants us to see sin as a closed case, never to be reopened or reconsidered by Him again.

And God calls Jesus our advocate or, even more lucid, our defense attorney. He is the One who pleads our case for us.

Picture a courtroom. You are the defendant, Jesus is your counsel, God is the judge, and Satan, the accuser of the brethren, is the prosecuting attorney. You are a believer, and Satan just saw you transgress the law. He says, "Look here, God. Here's Your big holy saint. Here's the person You said was blameless, the justified one, the one robed with righteousness. Look what he just did!"

Jesus immediately steps before the bench and says, "Father, You and I agreed together before the foundations of the world that My shed and sprinkled blood included payment for this sin, as well as all others. I have already paid for it, the sin has been placed on My account, and it is marked 'paid in full.'"

God raps the gavel and says, "Acquitted! Case dismissed. Next case."

In His sight, this courtroom scene took place just once, and you have been awarded the decision with finality. You cannot come to trial again. Jesus Christ frees you from the curse, to live in goodness and power under His good government.

In 1 John 2:2 Jesus is the propitiation or the mercy seat. It is He who covers our sins from the wrath of God. We stand as righteous in Him! We are also told that He is the mercy seat for the whole world. (That is what propitiation means.) God is not even keeping score on the world. All sin was dealt with at Calvary.

In Christ, we have fellowship with the Father through His Holy Spirit in the church. Our sins are forgiven. We are membered together with other people who walk in agreement with Him. What an incredible freedom!

If you are not sure you know Christ, why not at this moment

turn from yourself and your inadequacy and accept Him as your Lord and Savior? Tell Him you are relying on Him and His provision for your sins and that you wish for Him to be your life. Simply thank Him for what He has done in your behalf. Thank Him that He will start you out fresh again in life, making you the kind of person He wants for His kingdom.

With John, I can say, "I am writing to you . . . because your sins are forgiven you for His name's sake."[3]

The Lord thy God in the midst of thee is mighty; he will save, he will rejoice over thee with joy; he will rest in his love, he will joy over thee with singing.   Zephaniah 3:17

5. Love Is First

The words "Christian responsibility" often come through to me as a misnomer. They generally are employed to describe something I must do if I am going to be a Christian. I would much prefer the term "Christian response." A response is a spontaneous act resulting from a specific stimulus. I "respond" to Jesus Christ, but I tend to get burdened down by thinking I have a "responsibility" toward Him. I mean, how could I possibly, as a mortal being, assert myself as *ever* having fulfilled my responsibility to the God of the universe? It's presumptuous. Allowing me to respond to Him makes me feel free, but telling me I have a responsibility to Him makes me feel terribly in bondage.

This is where we need to grab hold of the fact that God's love comes ahead of everything else.

I feel the same way about the word *commitment*. I still use it because it has taken on a generic meaning, but I do not like it. In its usual context the word tends to mean that which I do to give myself to God, and it is generally interpreted as being causal in the relationship. We hear the phrase, "You ought to be more committed." Let me ask a question. *How* can I get more committed? What do I *do* to get more committed? If I understand the Word of God correctly, it is not my commitment, but His love, which initiates our oneness.

At the same time, let me say I have never sensed a greater commitment on my part to Christ and His church than I do right now. I'd die for Him and His people, and my life is as given over to the kingdom of God as I can knowingly will it to be. But my sense of dedication has nothing whatever to do with trying to merit His love and goodness to me. The dedication and commitment have been *put* in my heart, placed there by the Holy Spirit.

I am sorry if what I say sounds bothersome or unnecessary. Maybe I just had to say it for my own benefit, to get it off my chest. But I spend a great portion of my time out among fellow Christians who are doing their absolute best to be "more responsible" and to achieve "greater commitment," and I hurt for them. For me, being responsible or being committed is no longer the issue. The whole concept has been placed in perspective over in the category of "natural responses."

God says that "we love Him, because He first loved us."[1] The starting point in our whole identity with Christ is the fact that God loves us. John 3:16 reinforces this truth. "For God so loved the world, that He gave His only begotten Son, that whoever believes in Him should not perish, but have eternal life." God's basic motivation toward us is His love. God loves us first. If He waited around for us to love Him first, He would still be waiting! Love is the first great cause of the universe. God is love. He does not just give love; He is love. Love is a part of the very essence of His being. Because He loves us, a relationship with Him is possible.

A few years ago, our family visited Daytona Beach over the Easter break, and I had an exciting time interacting with some of the thousands of college kids who were on the beach. One evening, it was my pleasure to meet a young man named Don, a senior at Rutgers University. As we talked, I asked him if he had ever placed his trust in Jesus Christ.

"I could never become a Christian," he said.

"Why not?" I asked.

"Because I'm an agnostic," he answered, just as sincere as he could be.

"Don, God loves the agnostics as much as He loves everybody else," I said.

Now, this sounds pedestrian to most of us, but it was music to Don's ears. He felt that in order to become a Christian he first needed to arrive at the philosophical position of rationally believing in the possibility of Jesus Christ being available to him. I explained to him that God loves us just as we are.

I wish I still had the letter I received from him a few weeks later. He had become a Christian and was engaged to marry a girl he had known for years — a girl who had been praying that he would come to know Christ.

It was the love of God — the realization that God loved him without any qualifications whatever — that drew him to the Savior.

God initiates His love to us without our ever doing one thing to merit His favor or concern. (In fact, it is quite clear that if we went on the merit system, we would merit His wrath.) In Ephesians 5:22-33 Paul compares the love God has for us with the love in human marriage. Throughout the entire passage, the husband is told repeatedly to love his wife the same way Christ loves the church and gave Himself for it. The wife, on the other hand, is told to be subject to her husband as the church is subject to Jesus as its head.

It is interesting to me that nowhere in this exhortation is the wife told to love her husband. The assumption is that she will love her husband as a response to his love for her. He initiates the love relationship; she responds.

In a courtship situation, a man does not seek a woman who will love him; he looks for a woman whom he can love. He is the head or the initiator of the love relationship. In a similar way, a woman does not look for a man she can love; she looks for a man to love her. She is created as a responder. And this is what helps make a marriage tick. God built the man as the initiator, the wife as the responder, and as he loves her, she, in turn, loves him.

Now, granted, that passage *does* say the wife is to be submissive to her husband. But can you imagine me coming home and saying, "Wife, submit!" That would produce the most awkward and tense situation in the world.

For example, I love my wife whether the house is immaculate or messy. I don't *demand* dinner at six, or that the kids are bathed and fed. She *wants* to please me because I love her. It is to my love that she responds best, not to cold directives.

Yet, how many of us picture God standing up in heaven yelling down to us, "Christian, submit!" Our view of God tends to center in His demands rather than in His love. It's difficult to fall in love with an authority figure, but it's easy to love one who loves you. Obviously God has authority over me; He made me. But to prove His love for me, He actually became a man and died for me that I might live. I wouldn't call that pulling authority, would you? He came to us with His love so that we, in turn, could volitionally respond to Him. And His love never wears thin.

The same is true in the human family. One day a friend asked, "Why do you love your kids?" I thought for a minute, and the only answer I could come up with was, "Because they're mine." They need do nothing to prove themselves to me. I take them just as they are. God feels the same way about us. He loves us as we are, and it is His love which motivates us to trust and obey Him in return. God's grace produces commitment.

You hear it said quite often in our contemporary world that if we can just become honest with each other, we will be able to identify in vital brotherhood with our fellow-man. The thought is that honesty can become the basis of relationship. But honesty comes as the result of love. It is impossible to engender love by simply establishing honesty. I think we all have been in enough "honesty sessions" to discover this. The Scriptures talk about "speaking the truth in love."[2] The truth, apart from love, can become biting and destructive. But where love forms the core of the relationship, honesty is one of the inherent by-products.

Psychologists tell us man has two basic needs: to love and to be loved. They're right, but the order should be reversed. According to the patterns of Scripture, we first must be loved; then we are capable of loving. The life of Jesus Christ bore the perfect example of this truth. His whole mission was to love us first. During His earthly life, He chose His disciples just as they were and initiated the relationship by love. He availed Himself to the poor and rich alike. Taking no thought for their status in life, He showed His love to them at the point of their need and met them where they were. He died for a nation that rejected Him and for a race that was oblivious of Him. In Romans we read, "For one will hardly die for a righteous man; though perhaps for the good man someone would dare even to die. But God demonstrates His own love toward us, in that while we were yet sinners, Christ died for us."[3]

God loves you as you are right now. He *is* love. If you have been a Christian a million years and have never done a thing for

Him, He still loves you as you are. We do not turn the love of God on and off by what we do. If you have heard the gospel ten thousand times and have willfully and angrily turned it down with fervent consistency, He still loves you.

It is here that people often ask, "Well, what about hell?" Many of us picture God as being One who delights in choosing up sides, sending some to heaven and some to hell. Somehow the idea has been adopted that everything was going all right until the time that Jesus visited the earth. But once He arrived, people had to make a choice, and thus the possibility of a life apart from God began to exist because of Christ and what He said.

God is not the One who has changed; it is man. In His love, God formed us and placed us here on earth to have dominion and to walk with Him in fellowship forever. It was man who became the variable and who stepped out on his own. Thus, estrangement occurred. Isaiah wrote, "But your iniquities have separated between you and your God, and your sins have hid his face from you, that he will not hear."[4] The separation began when we sinned. And God's love for us was so strong that He provided a way back to this fellowship and dominion we once enjoyed, if we wanted it. And the contact point of His love was the cross of Jesus Christ, His Son. The reunion did not come easily for Him. It cost Him His life.

It is interesting that on the Day of Atonement in the Old Testament, the priest had little choice but to enter into the Holy of Holies to perform the sacrifice. Even if no one else in all of Israel cared about what he was doing, his motive for sacrifice went beyond them. He had sins of his own. He brought the blood "for himself and for the sins of the people. . . ."[5] Jesus, on the other hand, had no reason whatsoever to die for us, other than that He loved us so much. He had everything to lose and nothing to gain. He had no sin problems at all. His life was laid down *strictly* for our benefit.

And if I had been the only one on all the earth to die for, He still would have loved me enough to sacrifice Himself in my stead. It is this, His love, which so greatly motivates me to love Him back and to allow Him the control and Lordship of my life.

So all of us, apart from Christ, were living in estrangement from God. Hell is simply that estrangement drawn out for all eternity. I have heard people say they are experiencing a hell on earth, and I don't argue with them. What they are really communicating is that they are experiencing separation from God in *this* life. Hell is merely a continuation of that estrangement in the next life. The thing that makes hell hell is not the fire and brimstone, though Jesus made it clear these elements would exist. Hell is hell primarily because God is not there; it is solitary confinement away from Him for ever and ever. And even my natural mind in all its sadistic morbid blackness could never think of anything worse.

Jesus Christ, God's love personified, seeks to rescue us out of this eternal mess. Because of our sin, we are already *in* it. He is not trying to send us to hell; we are all its citizens as it is. His plan is to take all the "whosoever will may comes" out of this godless disarray so that we might be one with Him right now and be fully restored to His eternal purpose. And when people glow over their happiness being as "heaven on earth," it becomes far clearer what they mean. They have passed from death into life and are enjoying every minute of their restored relationship with Christ, as citizens of His new nation.

Jesus loves you right this instant. There is no reason to be afraid of Him or of His will as you trust Him. Perfect love casts out fear.[6] He's *for* you.

Yea, I have loved thee with an everlasting love: therefore with lovingkindness have I drawn thee.   Jeremiah 31:3

6.   Love Is Unconditional

Because God loved us first, He also loves us unconditionally. God does not say, "I love you if . . . ." He says, "I love you." Period.

In all of secular or religious literature, nothing has ever been penned on the subject of love which even closely rivals God's inspired masterpiece in 1 Corinthians 13. Men from all ages within the last two millenniums have paid homage to its peerless expression. Many people read the chapter daily. Evangelist Billy Graham says it is his favorite passage in the entire Bible.

1. If I speak with the tongues of men and of angels, but do not have love, I have become a noisy gong or a clanging cymbal.
2. And if I have the gift of prophecy, and know all

  mysteries and all knowledge; and if I have all faith, so as to remove mountains, but do not have love, I am nothing.

3. And if I give all my possessions to feed the poor, and if I deliver my body to be burned, but do not have love, it profits me nothing.

4. Love is patient, love is kind, and is not jealous; love does not brag and is not arrogant,

5. does not act unbecomingly; it does not seek its own, is not provoked, does not take into account a wrong suffered,

6. does not rejoice in unrighteousness, but rejoices with the truth;

7. bears all things, believes all things, hopes all things, endures all things.

8. Love never fails; but if there are gifts of prophecy, they will be done away; if there are tongues, they will cease; if there is knowledge, it will be done away.

9. For we know in part, and we prophesy in part;

10. but when the perfect comes, the partial will be done away.

11. When I was a child, I used to speak as a child, think as a child, reason as a child; when I became a man, I did away with childish things.

12. For now we see in a mirror dimly, but then face to face; now I know in part, but then I shall know fully just as I also have been fully known.

13. But now abide faith, hope, love, these three; but the greatest of these is love.

I can remember hearing sermons on 1 Corinthians 13 ever since I was old enough to sit still for a half-hour to listen to a speaker, and I would say to myself, "That is correct; I need to love more," but nothing ever happened to make me love more. When I received Jesus Christ into my life, I found a new desire to love others, and sometimes really did. I was more acutely aware of my need to love people as they were. But just *how* to let go and express the love was difficult. Oftentimes I did not experience love for others, and I knew the answer was in

Christ, but I could never seem to get it all the way down from Him to me.

Orations on the theme of love usually took somewhat predictable paths in their intent. The most common challenge was, "You must love others more because it's the Christian thing to do." It was back on the old responsibility kick again. Agreeing that the thesis was correct was no problem; how to perform it in everyday life was. The next most common dimension of application from 1 Corinthians 13 was, "You and I are incapable of loving others. Therefore, admit your incapacity to God, and let Jesus love others *through* you." That was the route I chose to take.

Either there was something wrong with Jesus Christ or I had a clogged tube somewhere, but whatever it was, there were many people who were not being loved by Christ through me.

Then I heard a slightly different slant on the matter: It isn't so much that He loves other *people* through you; it is the Christ *in* them which is the object of His love. Now I really felt I'd lost my identity. Christ in me loving Christ in you? That's doubletalk! If He didn't need *me*, but just used me as a channel, and if He didn't need other people, except to the extent they provided free housing for Him, what in the world were we here for? Regardless of what was meant by these reflections on love, none of them seemed to work.

Today I'm so excited about love I can hardly sit still. I sprouted no wings, I have not enrolled for harp lessons, and I have not become sinless. I do not love 100 percent of the people 100 percent of the time. But I got locked in with a small group of Christian friends over the course of one summer and learned love — both by experience and through God's written Word.

Traditionally we have limited the application of 1 Corinthians 13 to mean the way we are supposed to love other people. In our consideration of the passage, I would like to use it as a basic description of how *God* loves *us*. And that's valid. Would it be fair, after all, for God to tell you and me to love others in a way He hasn't first loved us? That would make the creature greater than the Creator. And as we have already discussed, God *is* love. Therefore He must love us *at least* as much as love is revealed in 1 Corinthians 13. Let us consider a few portions of that chapter.

LOVE IS PATIENT

God is *so* patient toward us. Often we get impatient with ourselves, and we do this because we honestly believe God is impatient with us. But God is extremely patient because love is patient, and God is love. We look at our lives and say to ourselves, "I'm not growing fast enough. I don't do enough for the Lord." Or even, "I don't love Him enough."

How much is enough? There is no *enough*. But He is patient and accepts the love you do give Him. He loves you where you are in your spiritual development. And it is knowing this that frees you to move ahead toward greater faith and obedience without the limitations of past performance.

One day I was sitting at my desk when our four-year-old walked through the room trying to thread a needle. If you have never witnessed a small child threading a needle, or attempting to do so, you are in for one of life's great frustrating experiences. The end of the thread was blunt and frazzled, and the needle in her other hand was turned sideways and unsteady in her grasp. My inclination was to snatch it away from her and do it myself. Watching her miss the target over and over again was like listening to a musical number with a dissonant ending; you want to rush to the piano and play the resolving chord so your soul might rest in peace.

As I watched her, I started to think about the number of times God must want to interrupt what I'm doing and do it

Himself. But He is patient. I decided to let her keep trying. Finally, she said, "Daddy, would you do it for me?" I exhaled with satisfaction and relief, took the needle and thread, wet and twisted the thread, inserted it though the needle's eye, and returned it to her. She thanked me and proceeded to play.

Sometimes the Lord lets us get to the end of our ropes on a project or ambition because He loves us too much to interfere. If he were to intervene, we would never learn. But once I have tried and failed and then give it to Him, I know the next time to trust Him with it from the start. God's love is patient, and His patience with me allows me to discover for myself that I can trust Him completely.

Love Is Kind

Kindness is not my personal forte, but God is so kind to me. Kindness means being considerate and not taking advantage of others — not kicking a person when he's down.

Knowing the kindness of our Father has been especially meaningful, for somehow I had acquired the concept of a God who gets even. My view of Him was that as long as I did what I knew was right, fine. But the second I failed, God would not only push the consequences on me, but He would continue to rain dirt upon me until I got back on my feet. The apostle Paul speaks heavily to me: "Or do you think lightly of the riches of His kindness and forbearance and patience, not knowing that the kindness of God leads you to repentance?"[1] It is His kindness that encourages me to change my mind about sin, forsake it as evil, and follow Christ whatever the cost.

Here was the prodigal son.[2] He grew up in a fine Jewish home and had everything a person could desire. One day he was doing some elementary math out behind the barn. He figured, "Why wait around till I'm old and wrinkled to latch on to my inheritance, when I could be out living it up while I'm still young enough to enjoy it."

He stopped by the house for his share of the money and took off for town. Soon he was behind on payments on his chariot, owed a bill at the inn, had lost some money on the market, and was out of ready cash. Tragedy of tragedies, he had to go to work for a living. After waiting in line at the local employment office, he finally landed a job slopping garbage to the hogs for a free bed and leftovers from what the swine didn't want. This was Jewish skid row — the idea of being penned in with those unclean beasts! The painful circumstances finally jolted him to his senses, and, after agreeing he was wrong and was willing to make restitution, he headed for home.

Instead of putting his son through the third degree, that father, it says, loved him and "ran and embraced him."[3] He received him with kindness. The lad had learned his lesson. Discipline in this case would have been redundant.

God is not out to get people when they're down. He wants to help them up. Love is kind, and God is love.

LOVE IS NOT PROVOKED

The King James Version of the Bible says, "Love is not *easily* provoked," but the word *easily* is not in the text. God just plain is not provoked; His anger has been satisfied at Calvary. All of the wrath that should have fallen on us came upon the Lord Jesus Christ. His reason for being provoked with us was our sin and unbelief. It was these which Jesus bore. If a person chooses to disbelieve Jesus Christ and strike out on his own, then His sacrifice is, for him, null and void. The cross dealt with sin, and the price for sin has been paid. The issue for us is not so much good versus evil as it is life versus death. The barrier which kept us from life has been broken down. Jesus said, "Truly, truly, I say to you, he who hears My word, and believes Him who sent Me, has eternal life, and does not come into judgment, but has passed out of death into life."[4] Therefore, sin is out of the way, and life is our live option.

In Christianity it's not what you know but whom you know. If we reject Jesus, the unique source of satisfaction for the wrath of God, then, by choice, we are stuck with what's left. Wrath is a part of death; love is a part of life. God has done everything He can possibly do to solve our problems of sin and guilt. To quote Jesus, "It is finished."[5] If we turn Him down, we are saying to Him that we choose to believe it would never work. Thus John was forced to conclude the third chapter of his Gospel by saying, "He who believes in the Son has eternal life; but he who does not obey the Son shall not see life, but the wrath of God abides on him."[6]

LOVE DOES NOT TAKE INTO ACCOUNT A WRONG SUFFERED

An account is a list or a ledger, and a wrong suffered is a sin. As of A.D. 33, God deals with neither. Paul said that "God was in Christ reconciling the world to Himself, not counting their trespasses against them . . . ."[7] God *has dealt* with wrongs suffered, as He promised, and no longer takes them into account.[8]

I was speaking in a church one Sunday, and after the service a woman approached me and said, "How does what you say fit in with the fact that God takes into account every idle word?"

"I'm not sure," I replied. "Let's look it up and see." In thinking through the riches of the grace of God, I had forgotten some of the passages in the Gospels that appeared to be inconsistencies. We found the passage in question in Matthew 12 and read it in context:

34. You brood of vipers, how can you, being evil, speak what is good? For the mouth speaks out of that which fills the heart.
35. The good man out of his good treasure brings forth what is good; and the evil man out of his evil treasure brings forth what is evil.

36. And I say to you, that every careless word that men
    shall speak, they shall render account for it in the day
    of judgment.
37. For by your words you shall be justified, and by your
    words you shall be condemned.

Jesus was speaking here to a group of men who were vehement in their opposition to Him. They were not believers at all. And as He conversed with them, He made it clear that the only way to speak righteous words was to be righteous on the inside. Idle or careless words, on the other hand, were simply evidences of unbelief.

This did two things for me. Negatively, it made me breathe easier over idle words I had spoken. They were forgiven. Positively, God showed me that because I am indwelt with the life of Christ, righteous words will emerge from me as a result. Consequently, I've found myself having fewer problems with careless words.

LOVE DOES NOT REJOICE IN UNRIGHTEOUSNESS

Several years ago I was riding with a friend through downtown Indianapolis during rush hour. There was no on-the-street parking allowed in the business section of that city from three to six P.M. due to the heavy traffic. It was about 3:45. As we were cruising down one of the main streets of town, about two blocks ahead I could see a tow truck back up in front of a huge Mercedes-Benz. The winch slowly lowered, and the driver got out of the truck and came around between the two vehicles to hook them together. About the time we drove past the scene, the car had been hoisted up by the chain, and we could see the truck start up and head down the street behind us, towing its prey.

I howled with laughter. That was one of the most satisfying sights I had seen in years. The reason for my hilarity was that a few years earlier that same thing had happened to me in a *No*

Parking 4-6 zone in Minneapolis. And it was *so* good to see it happen to somebody else.

That is rejoicing in unrighteousness. God doesn't do that. His source of joy is in the truth. God does not even delight when the devil pushes his own people around. Happiness for God is to see an unbeliever turn to Christ and receive new life. Our Father is so lovely and gracious; He never thinks in terms of evening up the score. He is merciful even to our iniquities![9]

LOVE BELIEVES ALL THINGS

We have been told over and over again to believe in God, and that is as it should be. But God wants us to know He believes in us. Love believes all things, and God is love.

For years, people told me I did not have the ability to write. One man, for whom I worked, sat me down in his office one afternoon and said to me, "Pete, you just don't have the stuff." I wasn't heartsick over it because whether I could or could not write made little difference to me. I had some other plans which didn't necessarily include journalism.

Later an editor of a well-known magazine told me that he felt I had some definite potential in the area of writing. A friend in the publishing business actually *encouraged* me to write, and said it with enthusiasm at that. The result is this book.

My purpose in writing is to get a message out. I do not feel I am especially talented in communicating per se. But the fact that a few people believed in me motivated me to get busy.

God really believes in you! He believes you are a new person, if you have come to know Jesus Christ. He has little confidence in the old you — what you were before you accepted Him — but He knows that now you can do all things through Christ, who is your strength.[10] He does not expect you to fail. If you do, He still loves and forgives you. But He assumes you will persevere because He has given you all things you will ever need relative to life and godliness.[11] If there were anything else He felt you needed or that He could have supplied you with, He would have done it. But as far as God is concerned, you have *got* to make it because you have *Him!*

I have a friend who used to live in Boston. He did not see the number of people trust in Christ that others saw in the same type of situation, but those he reached were all faithful. One day I said, "Doug, why is it so many of my converts seem to fall by the wayside, while most of yours go on?" His reply was, "I don't *let* them fall. I expect every one to keep moving." Later, I talked with some of his men. The thought of unfaithfulness to the Lord had never crossed their minds.

God believes in you. Not just because He is good at thinking positive thoughts (though I'm sure He is), but because you are now a part of His family; He *owns* you! If we count on this, we are free from the worry that comes from uncertainties in relationships. There are no uncertainties as far as God is concerned. Jesus said He would never leave you nor forsake you.[12]

LOVE NEVER FAILS

We see that saying on dusty plaques in parlors of old homes. But, wow, is it true! Love *never* fails. *God* never fails. He never fails to love you first. He never fails to love you unconditionally. He never fails to be patient, kind, etc., etc., etc. He is on duty in your behalf twenty-four hours a day.

*For the whole Law is fulfilled in one word, in
the statement, "You shall love your neighbor
as yourself."*   Galatians 5:14

7. You Can
Love Yourself

The end result of God's love flowing unconditionally from Him
to us is that a love response is activated within our lives. His
love becomes creative; it molds us into new persons. God's
love does not *demand* a change; it *produces* one.

The passage "We love, because He first loved us"[1] tells the
whole story of the creative love cycle. But there is something
between our receiving God's love and, in turn, giving it back to
Him that is tremendously important. It is this in-between step
that we wish to consider here.

Way back in Sunday school almost all of us, regardless of our
denominational backgrounds, learned a little adage that went
something like this:

> Jesus first,
> Others second,
> Yourself third.

77

It was a convenient and easy slogan because the first three letters of those phrases spelled *joy*, and kids found it easy to remember. But the divine order of that saying should go:

> Jesus loves me first,
> I love myself because He loves me,
> Now that I love myself, I am free to love others.

(That will never sell because, first, it's too long, and, second, it spells *jin* which says nothing. However, this "new order" is correct.)

Before I can address myself to the challenge of loving or accepting other people as they are, I must first take *myself* as I am. And before the latter is possible, I need to know *God* loves me as I am.

Jesus said, "Love your neighbor just as you love yourself," or, applied conversely, "Before you can love your neighbor, you must be able to love yourself." In fact, as Tom Skinner says, "If you can't love yourself, your neighbor is in big trouble!"

We get all hot and bothered about this thing of loving ourselves. Since the psychologists came on the scene with the ego bit, most of us Christians have pulled our heads back into our shells and started hating ourselves because, suddenly, ego is bad. But in conversion, my ego acquires a forwarding address. I am no longer under the domain of the flesh; I am now controlled by the Holy Spirit. The real me is a new person; I have been reborn.

Loving ourselves is crucial to loving others — even God! Paul came right out and said it in describing love on the human plane in the context of marriage. "So husbands ought also to love their own wives as their own bodies. He who loves his own wife loves himself."[3] It's the age-old principle that before I can straighten out other people's houses, I'd better get my own in order. If loving doesn't work at home, it surely will not work with others.

What does it mean to love ourselves? Basically, it is to see ourselves as God sees us. The trouble is, we traditionally say that God sees us as dirty, rotten sinners, and we stop right there. God sees us as dirty, rotten, *forgiven and restored* sinners! He looks at us as part of His new creation, part of the new man, vessels unto honor, uniquely His, meet for the Master's use.[4] His word to personal sin is, "and such were some of you."[5] He is satisfied with us because His Son presents us faultless before Him. In His sight we are winners, not losers; overcomers, not overcome; we are a kingdom of priests unto God.[6]

Loving ourselves also involves accepting our weaknesses as well as our strengths. I, personally, stormed into the kingdom of God with, among other things, a bad temper. Now that is sin, and I have called it such before the Lord. But rather than hate myself because of this weakness, I have come to accept it as something the Lord and I are dealing with. This is not to say my temper is right, but it is to say God took me that way and forgave me. Since I accept my temper problem, I am free to accept yours. That has changed my life. If I inwardly curse myself when I lose my cool, I will inevitably do the same thing to you when you lose yours. But if I do not condemn myself over my temper problem, but instead turn from it, I will allow you the same privilege. I am learning to accept myself as I am and others as they are. And the beauty of it is, that as I turn my attention from myself and my problems to Jesus Christ and His sufficiency, I have fewer anger problems. My temper no longer threatens me, because it's not the issue; Jesus Christ is.

Some friends in Kansas call this "relaxing in the Spirit," and they are right. We have been liberated by the death and resurrection of Jesus Christ to take ourselves as we are and let

Him cleanse us. And He is *so* much better at that sort of thing than we are.

And before I get off this matter of self-acceptance, I want to mention the physical ramifications, too. Some of us are downright ugly. We look in the mirror in the morning and whisper to God, "How come You didn't make me good-looking? I've seen a better face on a watch."

God made us as we are for a reason. He could best be glorified in us that way. Listen to what King David says in Psalm 139 as he ponders God's feelings for His created individual:

> 13. For thou didst form my inward parts, thou didst knit me together in my mother's womb.
> 14. I praise thee, for thou art fearful and wonderful. Wonderful are thy works! Thou knowest me right well;
> 15. my frame was not hidden from thee, when I was being made in secret, and intricately wrought in the depths of the earth.
> 16. Thy eyes beheld my unformed substance; in thy book were written, every one of them, the days that were formed for me, when as yet there was none of them.
> 17. How precious to me are thy thoughts, O God! How vast is the sum of them! (RSV)

In Ephesians, Paul says much the same thing about God's new creation, and the principle is identical. "For we are His workmanship, created in Christ Jesus for good works, which God prepared beforehand, that we should walk in them."[7] The word *workmanship* in the Greek is the word *poetry*.

Has anyone ever told you that when they made you they threw away the mold? It always draws a laugh when it's said in a crowd. But poetry is not made from a mold; it's a totally creative act. There has never been another person like you and there never will be. And your soul and your spirit are unique as well. God loves you as you are.

When I was in high school, I always wanted to be physically big. I was 6'4'' but weighed only 145. I was so slender that after gym class I had to *run around* in the shower in order to get wet! It was the style back then to wear a V-neck sweater with only a T-shirt underneath. Since I would turn sideways and disappear, I wore three or four T-shirts under my sweater just to pork up enough to be seen. My weight (or my lack of it) began to affect the real me because I did not accept myself as I was. I was down on God because I was not heavier.

Because God loves me and created me as I am — body, soul, spirit — I am able, through knowing Him, to accept and be thankful for myself the way I am. (Now I've been adding some pounds, so this illustration may soon be invalid!)

During a recent trip to Memphis, I became engaged in an in-depth conversation with a good friend who is from Atlanta. He is somewhat younger than I and is very much interested in and contemplative of the idea of marriage.

"I am ready to fall in love and settle down," he said, "but I don't really trust myself. I have this basic fear that I will meet a girl who is everything I want, fall in love, but then, at a later time, meet someone else I really feel is better. It is because of this fickleness of my own heart that marriage tends to scare me off."

The subject of marriage is one of my favorites. There has probably never been a mortal soul more enthusiastic over the institution of marriage than I. And I am very closed-minded on the subject. I feel I ended up with the best, most beautiful, most lovable girl in the whole world.

"Tom," I remarked to my friend, "I can see what you mean, but that thought has never presented itself to me as a possibility. I accept Marilyn as she is, and she takes me as I am. We want only each other. She loves me with all my faults and inadequacies, and I love her with hers. And our love creates in each other a deeper and broader capacity to love. Instead of our affection waning or remaining static, it just keeps growing."

We turned to the passage in Ephesians 5 regarding loving our wives as our own bodies. "Let me ask you a question," I said. "Do you feel there are other guys in the world better looking than you?"

"Of course," he replied, laughing.

I mentioned the name of a close, mutual friend who is regarded by most people as very handsome. "Is he better equipped physically than you?"

Tom agreed right away that he was.

"Let me ask — whose body would you rather have, yours or his?"

"I'd rather have mine," he said.

"Why?"

"I'm not sure," he said. "I just like it."

We both chortled at ourselves for talking this way. I don't think either of us had ever verbalized these thoughts before.

"Now," I continued, "say that you fall deeply in love with a wonderful girl. She is wild about you. You see her faults and don't care. You love her anyway. She is aware of your flaws, but that doesn't matter to her in the least. She loves you beyond all that. God gives you peace about the relationship and you become one — man and wife. She is now yours. She *belongs* to you. She and you have become one flesh. Her love thrills you past description. And you discover the love you give to her delights her immensely. She tells you so.

"Now in the course of everyday life you will meet thousands of other women. But, Tom — and this is basic — whose body do you want; to which person do you feel continually drawn?"

"Man, I've never thought about that before," he answered. "You really *do* love your wife like you love yourself. She is a part of you."

Love is so creative. It provides a security pocket out of which you never want to escape. The thought of closing out on Jesus

Christ has never been in my mind since I became a Christian. We have a love thing going that is so much better than *anything* else. He has created within me a desire to be with Him forever. The thought of snooping around for a new marriage partner is equally irrelevant. Other women will be winning beauty contests and charm awards from now till Armageddon. That doesn't bait me a bit. I've got something going for me that's so strong, I am scarcely aware of any kind of option or alternative.

According to government statistics, divorce in this country is at an all-time high. In many cities and counties divorces outnumber marriages. People do not know how to love each other. Apart from a spiritual birth, God's kind of love is impossible to see and understand. The world says, "You love me first, then I'll love you. But my love will stop if you do not do what I say." All the natural man has to go on are performance-centered relationships. Since people are rarely accepted on any basis other than what they do, they have no alternative orientation by which to accept others. The disease spreads from the individual to society. And the world-system is born. In this system, unconditional, undemanding love cannot work because the entire structure of society militates against it.

Part of salvation is being saved *out* of the world. The church is a brand-new society. It is part of God's kingdom, and love is what holds the kingdom together. Marriage, too, is a product of that kingdom. That is why marriage often does not and cannot work in the world. It is out of its natural element. We have tried to transplant it from the kingdom back into the world, and we do not succeed.

When a husband, as a person, and a wife, as a person, are born of God and know Him, they *experience* His perfect love. They know that it comes by grace, not by merit. They believe they are constantly abiding in forgiveness, and their actions form no obstruction to their oneness with God. It is here where they can then accept themselves. They accept their flaws and their weaknesses because God does, and through the power of the Holy Spirit they will turn from them. They find as they forget their failures, as God already has, and simply walk with Him, these liabilities will tend to disappear. And as they love and accept themselves without condemnation, they are capable of loving and accepting each other the same way — God's way!

Which of these two situations would keep me more faithful to my wife? If, before I embark on a short journey, she were to say to me, "I love you, but you better not cheat on me while you're gone." Or if she would say, "My love for you is so deep that even if you were to turn from me, my love would not alter one bit!"

Those words need never be articulated. It's the heart attitude that says it. But as we know and feel God's love for us, from Him through the cross of Christ and from others through the body of Christ, a new life of love will be *created* in us. First Corinthians 13 will become our life. It will work in our own lives, in our love for God, and in our love for others.

And an highway shall be there, and a way,
and it shall be called The way of holiness; the
unclean shall not pass over it; but it shall be
for those: the wayfaring men, though fools,
shall not err therein.   Isaiah 35:8

If therefore the Son shall make you free, you
shall be free indeed.   John 8:36

8.   The Road to Freedom

God's love not only makes possible the complete cleansing of our lives, allowing us a fresh, new confidence before Him, but He also declares us free and unshackled from the law. Through Christ we have been removed from the monotonous, tiring trails of performance and religious effort and placed upon what Isaiah the prophet called the "highway of holiness." It is a spacious, scenic, and, unfortunately, seldom-traveled road to freedom.

Aside from the engulfing de-emphasis upon the grace and forgiveness of God and the reign of the Spirit in the church (to be discussed in chapter 9), if I had to name the next greatest plague upon Christendom today it would have to be that we as believers have forgotten we've been declared free people.

We who call ourselves Christians have become entwined

with behavior-centered as opposed to belief-centered relationships to Christ, and those who exist without the gates of God's earthly reign are kept from Him by our oft-told insistence upon "Christian conformity."

WHY THE GOOD NEWS IS SO GOOD!

A small group of us were addressing the members of a prominent social fraternity at UCLA. After the meeting, among several men who expressed their interest in knowing Jesus Christ was one young man who insisted he meet with someone in our group who would be available just as soon as possible.

Over coffee the following morning, he said, "I would give my eyeteeth to have what you men have. But there's one thing holding me back."

"What's that?" my friend replied.

"Witnessing," he said.

"What do you mean?" we asked.

"I know good and well if I give my heart to Christ, I'll have to start telling everyone I know how to get saved," he muttered.

"Where did you get that idea?" we inquired.

"It's no idea. Some people I know who are Christians told me so. They said if you trust Christ, that's part of your responsibility, along with praying, reading the Bible, going to —"

"Just a minute," my friend interrupted. "God says He takes us as we are. It's strictly a matter of trusting Him. There are no price tags attached."

"Aw, come on," he objected. "You guys are out witnessing. What do you mean, you don't have to?"

"We're doing it because we *want* to. It's a tremendous thing to share the life of Christ with people, but that doesn't have a thing to do with becoming a Christian."

We went on to explain to him the greatness of God's love and how at the cross Jesus Christ so totally removed the barriers between him and God that even if there were something he wanted to do to help deserve it, he couldn't.

"Are you telling me I could accept Jesus Christ right now and not have to do a thing in return, and He'd still accept me?" he inquired, almost puzzled.

We assured him that was so.

"Well, if you *promise* me Christ will come into my life today and I'll never have to witness, I'll accept Him."

"We promise," came our reply.

We prayed together, and he invited Jesus Christ to become his Lord and Savior. We went on to explain to him that God had forgiven all sin — past, present, and future — everything he ever had or ever would do was placed upon Jesus Christ. We told him about his new life that would never end.

"This is the most fantastic thing I have ever heard," he responded. "I can't believe that I didn't have to do anything to get it."

He walked back over to the fraternity house. It was about 10:00 in the morning. He approached the first friend he saw and said, "I've got to tell you the most amazing thing I have ever heard. Today I realized I could invite Jesus Christ to come into my life, and I wouldn't have to witness or do anything, and He'd still come in. This is the greatest thing I have ever heard. Isn't that fantastic!" And by evening, he had spread the word around the entire fraternity. Because he didn't *have* to.

When are we going to learn that righteousness comes not by works but by faith?

I visit different churches in my travels Sunday after Sunday, and nine times out of ten the message is: "We must pray more; how many hours of devotions have you had this week? Will you say a word for Christ at the office this week? Is your giving current?" And what we really need is *life*. Instead, death prevails, and the people leave — friendly, saying good-by, shaking hands, but immaculately unchanged.

TWO COMPONENTS OF SIN

Paul writes to this whole issue of law and grace throughout his epistles. In Romans 7 his descriptions and applications of the futility of law-giving are so graphic. He teaches, "For while we were in the flesh, the sinful passions, which were aroused by the Law, were at work in the members of our body to bear fruit for death" (Rom. 7:5).

This passage mentions two elements necessary for sin to be produced: *sinful passions* and *the law*. Sinful passion is the seat of rebellion within us, the thing about us that deep-down enjoys doing wrong. The law, on the other hand, serves as the object against which the sinful passions rebel. And, of course, it is not simply against the law of God that we rebel; it is against "law as a principle" as well.

There is a difference between law as a principle of living and the Old Testament law. The Old Testament written law has been fulfilled in Christ. However, Christians find themselves bothered by law as a principle — that is, man-made law. And both kinds of law — God's law and man's law — arouse rebellion in the hearts of people because of sin.

A family builds a beautiful new home just across the street, the entire front of which is plate glass. Other than admiring the home, nobody thinks much more about it. Then one day a man on the opposite side of town builds a home exactly like it, with the front constructed of plate glass. But he puts a sign out on his front lawn which warns, "Please do not throw stones through this window." Whose window will be broken first?

Or, you are on vacation in a secluded wooded area near a lake. On your first afternoon out, you take a walk along the shore and come upon a long dock going out into the water. At the far end of the dock is a sign which says NO FISHING FROM THE DOCK. You picture absolute whales swimming underneath, defying you to catch them. "The man who put up this sign wants them all to himself," you rationalize. And the presence of the sign triggers rebellion within you, tempting you to return to the car for your fishing gear.

Be it the law of God or the principle of law, man, because of his passion for sin, sets out to disobey. Paul himself says, "I would not have come to know sin except through the Law; for I would not have known about coveting if the Law had not said, 'You shall not covet'" (Rom. 7:7). The law energizes our capacity to sin; it turns our sin passions on, live and in color. And the apostle states that he came to know sin, in this case coveting or lusting, because the law said, "Don't do it."

Paul goes on to say, "But sin, taking opportunity through the commandment, produced in me coveting of every kind; for apart from the Law sin is dead" (Rom. 7:8). What a statement! Why is it that sin is produced in us? Just as when I, as an earthly father, say "No-no" to my child, and he goes ahead and does it anyway, so God says "no" to us and He gets a similar response. The problem is not that God or we are wrong in issuing the orders. The breakdown occurs within the human heart; the sin passions rebel and people do it anyhow!

The Better Idea

What is the solution? To let my child become lawless? Not at all. And that is not God's answer to the sin dilemma either. He has another plan. The Ford Motor Company announced one year, "Now, there's a better idea from Ford." God also made a similar announcement one year: "When He said, 'A new covenant,' He has made the first obsolete."[1] Now, there's a better idea from God!

"I will put My Laws into their minds, and I will write them upon their hearts."[2] Instead of the impersonal, demanding law from without, God's new plan is the personal and loving Holy Spirit from within.

I was visiting in the classroom of a well-known seminary not long ago, and the professor was teaching a course in Christian ethics. The subject of the day concerned God's giving of the law to Moses.

"Why was the law given?" the professor asked the class.

A hand went up in the front row. "To show us His standards of holiness," the student replied.

"Right," said the teacher. "Any other reasons?"

"God gave the law as a mirror for us to look into, so we would know we are sinful," a second student explained.

"Okay, that's good. Is there a third reason?" asked the professor.

No more hands went up. After a few moments of silence, I could resist no longer and raised my hand. "Can a visitor say a word?" I asked.

"Sure," said the professor.

"A third reason God gave the law was to make us sin more," I said.

Now there was *really* silence! Nobody said anything. Finally, the professor said, "I'm not sure I understand."

"Look up Romans 5:20," I suggested. (You have never heard such a flurry of page-turning in thirty different Bibles at the same time in your life!) The professor read aloud slowly and studiously:

"And the Law came in that the transgression might increase; but where sin increased, grace abounded all the more."

Then he read it aloud *all over again*.

"I've never seen that verse before," he said, re-reading it a third time silently to himself.

Part of the reason God put His people under law was that sin might increase. Paul wrote in another place, "The power of sin is the law."[3] Why in the world would God give something to the human race that would eventuate in further sin? Because through our misery and frustration of first, *wanting* to do better (we found out the difference between good and evil from the tree of the knowledge of good and evil in Genesis 3), and second, trying our best to be good and never meeting the expectations of either ourselves or God, we would call out to God in repentance and trust in His fulfillment of the law, Jesus Christ. In that sense, the law becomes our schoolmaster or personal tutor[4] which leads us to Christ.

God is fussy about this business of holiness. His standards are pure and absolute; there are no half-tones of gray. *Trying* to be holy, therefore, becomes doubly grave in its outcome. Even if we were to improve in our performance according to either man's or God's standards, it would never be good enough. So why waste our time and suffer the fatigue of failure in the arena of self-effort? Part of the purpose in Jesus' death and resurrection was to break us out of the penitentiary of human works and allow us to walk in His righteousness. If we insist on trying to obey static rules, we will sin all the more.

A man decides he is controlled by thoughts of lust and sets out to lick the problem. He gets up in the morning, and his first thoughts are, "Today, I will not lust. Today, I will not lust." He may even ask God's assistance. By mid-morning, he is so captured by his intentions against lusting that all he thinks about is lust. He becomes caught in his own trap.

The law just does not work as a *modus operandi* for living. But the Holy Spirit does. God never intended His commandments to produce holiness. He gave them to show us what holiness is and how those who are righteous should behave. But trying to adhere to the law of God as a means of attaining righteousness simply produces more sin.

Listen to what Paul declares in Romans 7:6: "But now we have been released from the Law, having died to that by which we were bound, so that we serve in newness of the Spirit and not in oldness of the letter." We are free people! Free to take our orders from the Holy Spirit as He leads us under the government of God.

Let me be as clear as I can be on a specific point: *when we say we are free from the law, we do not mean God has ceased issuing orders to His people.* After all, He is our King — and what king worth his salt does not give out commands to the people who serve under him? *Of course* God issues orders. As we noted a few pages back, He writes His laws on our hearts and on our minds. As people of His new covenant, His new agreement, the Holy Spirit speaks to our hearts and tells us what to do.

Under the old arrangement, God gave His commands to Israel on tablets of stone; under the new plan, the church receives its game plan written "on tablets of human hearts" by the Holy Spirit.[5] Do you see the fantastic difference? Through our spiritual eyes and ears we can see and hear from God as He gives out His special instructions through the Holy Spirit.

And because our hearts have been made soft and pliable through our new birth, instead of rebelling against the impersonal rules and regulations which were ours under the old plan, we now respond to the nudges and promptings of the Holy Spirit, walking in careful obedience to what He has to say.

A NEW SET OF WANT-TO'S

Further, there is a promise of God we cannot afford to overlook. The Scripture says, "Delight thyself also in the Lord; and he shall give thee the desires of thine heart."[6]

Let's take it back a step or two. In all my interaction with people, and I am talking now about those who do not claim to know Christ, I have never met a person whose true desire is to be evil. I speak constantly in college fraternities, to athletic teams, to business and social clubs, and I meet people who genuinely want to be changed. I am not saying that they are not morally decadent; they are. But they are looking for a way out! Individuals, for the most part, I believe, are not looking for ways to sin more and to get further into depression and guilt.

They are searching for a means of escape.

It is this "way out" that Jesus came to give. And the basic change He makes for most of us is not so much a new hunger for a *better* life, but rather a new possibility and power for a whole *new* life. Man has known the difference between good and evil all along, according to Romans 3. His lack has been the means of attainment.

So when Jesus Christ invades our hearts and lives, He comes to fulfill our desires, to give us the "desires of our hearts."

Let me ask, isn't your true desire to be a man or woman of God? Mine certainly is. That is not to say that my behavior is commensurate with that desire 100 percent of the time. But my true desire is to be righteous.

If you are a Christian and, being honest with yourself, you know you have a desire to break away and raise hell, your problem is most likely that you have been living under the law for so long that you've forgotten what walking by the directives of the Holy Spirit is really like.

It is here where we desperately need each other. To be free in Christ on a personal basis is mandatory, but there is more. I need the fellowship of other free men, that I might experience with them their freedom, and they mine. The check and balance for a child of God is not rules but relationships — with Him and with each other. We need one another experientially as brothers and sisters in Christ far more than we know, to encourage one another, to exhort and correct one another, to *be* that holy priesthood in which the Spirit of God has come to dwell.

We need to function together as living stones in the visible body of Christ.

Jesus makes us alive — alive to ourselves, to our real desires, to others, and to Him. He wasn't kidding about abundant life.[7] His great desire is that we might live life at its best: that our wills might be restored to oneness with His will.

I remember just after my own conversion how eager I was to know Christ better, in a deeper, more intimate way. Many of the people who told me about the joys of being a Christian, I observed, fellowshiped with Him in the Scriptures. So I deduced that I could learn of Him in this way, too.

I had a job that summer working nights in a commercial bakery. It would be 3:00 or so in the morning before I would get home. My usual practice was to hop in bed with my Bible and read it, often until the birds were singing or until it was light outside. Nobody ever told me to do this; I just did.

My growth spiritually was tremendous. God spoke to me with clarity and power during those early morning hours, and He used those times to give a foundation to my Christian life that was without parallel.

Later that summer I was invited to attend a two-week Christian conference. God taught me many valuable lessons during that time. One evening, however, a sincere, well-meaning speaker made this statement: "If you want to be a man of God, you must spend no less than one hour per day reading His Word."

I am a sensitive person at heart. And for sure, I wanted to be a man of God. So from that time on, for the next several months, I laboriously read the Bible. I made a grim attempt to stick with it an hour a day. Previously, I had often read for two, three, sometimes even four hours a day; now one hour was next to impossible. I would remove my wrist watch, lay it down on my desk, and time myself. Even if I completed the hour, I was learning virtually nothing. It had all become duty.

Then one day, someone dropped the line, "No Bible, no breakfast." "Alas," I thought, "here is my answer. If I just give God the opening hour of my day, my problems will be solved." But I am one of those people who don't wake up until two hours after they get out of bed. I got less out of the morning devotions than I did when I was gutting out an hour in the afternoon.

Next, I signed up for the "Read It Thru in '62" campaign in my church. It took me fifteen months, but I read it through — Genesis all the way to Revelation! But I can recall nothing that God taught me during that ordeal.

The final gimmick was trying to listen to the Bible on record. Invariably I fell asleep. My problem all along was that I had begun to view devotions as an "act" of being spiritual. And I was trapped.

It was not until I understood I was free from the law that my hunger for the Scriptures returned. I have never said this publicly, and I doubt I ever will, because in a book you can explain so much more than in a brief talk. But for three months I scarcely opened the Bible at all. Did God still bless? Yes. As strong as ever. Did the people I shared the gospel with respond during that period? Sure did! How about answered prayer? All kinds of it, in fact maybe more than at any other time in my life. How could God possibly allow a thing like . . . . It's called grace. I became so sick and tired of blasting through the Bible barrier that I quit reading it altogether. I had a "reentry problem" from law back to grace. I did not desire to read it, so I didn't. And life was beautifully abundant and free.

After three months — and this length of time was strictly uncalculated — my hunger for the Scriptures became so strong again, I could not resist reading them. Talk about happy — I was elated! It was the same joy I had known during my first weeks as a believer. Not because I stopped and then started again — and I don't recommend that route for *anyone* else — but because the Lord gave me the desires of my heart.

If you read the Bible faithfully each morning as a free man, I *urge* and *pray* that you continue. I do not share what I have learned to annoy you, but to perhaps help some frustrated believers, who are not like you, out from under their imitation holiness. If you have a systematic method of studying the Scriptures and God is teaching you and blessing you in your freedom, I admire your priceless gift of discipline. *Please* keep on studying. I do not have such a gift. But let's make a bargain. I won't ask people to do it my way, if you won't insist they do it yours!

Occasionally, I hear a statement something like this: "We are aware that we are free from the Old Testament law, but all of us know that we are responsible to obey the law of Christ." I have no contempt for those who say this, but I do feel it's putting the effect ahead of the cause. Obedience results from our relationship with Christ, as we have already noted, and is not the cause of it. If we truly are free, then ultimate righteousness will result. I believe we need to be patient and not instantly demand it from one another.

Another curious observation is this: If we were morally unable to keep and obey the law of Moses, how on earth will we ever obey the law of Christ, which is tougher? Moses said don't kill; Jesus said if we hate someone, we have killed him. Moses said do not commit adultery; Jesus said to not even give her the eye. If all of us were running around conscientiously determining to obey the law of Christ, we'd have folks with empty eye sockets, chopped-off hands, and the church would look like a huge amputation ward.

I want to stand on the housetops of orthodox Christendom and announce to men our freedom in the Lord Jesus. Sometimes I feel like throwing a celebration, just to get everybody together to thank Him for it. It cost Him His life, but He has set us free! He bled and died that freedom might be ours. We are free to be holy, free to *live*.

> Oh, God, please give us eyes to see that we can't please You, even as Your children, through works of righteousness that we do. Give us divine wisdom to believe You when You say that You will place Christ's righteousness within us as we simply depend upon Your Spirit to do so. Show us the meaning of Your statements: "You

shall know the truth, and the truth shall make you free,"[8] and "where the Spirit of the Lord is, there is liberty."[9] I pray, Father, as I write this that you will keep the devil from trying to convince fellow Christians who know they are bound up in the law to reject freedom in Christ as a brand of license and write it off as the meanderings of a young turk and thus return again to their molds of slavery to habit and routine defeat. May we see Jesus as He really is, ruling at the right hand of God, and ourselves as there with Him, members of His body.

Faithful is He who calls you, and He also will
bring it to pass.   1 Thessalonians 5:24

9.   How to Succeed in Christianity Without Really Trying

One evening during an outdoor political rally in Chicago, I joined a group of some thirty college students from the area to spend an evening in Lincoln Park talking with the visiting delegates and onlookers about Jesus Christ.

It was a typically warm and balmy August night in the Windy City, and an estimated 2,000 people were occupying the central portion of the park, many of them to voice their protests about the way things were developing in party politics. Some were intently involved in political discussion; the rest were milling around on the perimeter of the crowd, talking with one another.

Our group had met earlier on the other side of Lake Shore Drive to pray and interact on just how to begin sharing Christ with these people across the way. As we arrived in Lincoln

Park, I was somewhat confused as to what to do. I remember asking the Lord to somehow open things up for us to begin a conversation with one of the participants in the demonstration. A good friend, Don Berge, and I were together in a "two by two" arrangement.

We had been walking around the park for five minutes or so, when a young black student approached us. He seemed to be under the influence of some sort of stimulant, and I thought I smelled liquor on his breath. Standing right in front of me, he smiled and asked, "Anybody here got a high?"

"We've got a high that won't quit!" I responded.

"What's that?"

"The Holy Spirit," I said, unsure of what his reaction would be.

"You guys got the Holy Spirit?" he asked, with apparent sincerity.

"Sure do. How about you?"

"Naw, I don't," he replied. "But my grandmother did."

"Would you like to?"

"Yeah, I really would," he answered, far more serious and coherent.

Don and I began to relate to him how great it is to experience God's love and to personally count on His Son. He was interested in everything we said, and I was confident he wanted to know Christ. Just as we were explaining what receiving Jesus Christ is all about, a friend of his interrupted and quipped, "Brother, what you got?"

"Stay and listen," he said. "These dudes are talking about something we really need."

We backtracked in our conversation to include his friend, and before much time had passed both these young men were our brothers in Christ. The one we met first said later, "You don't know how glad I am you guys came by. These cats over here," he voiced with concern as he motioned to the crowd some fifty yards away, "don't really know where it's at."

The Holy Spirit really *is* a high that doesn't quit. He is more than just intermittent; He is new-life righteousness. No fix, no price, no withdrawal; just real, permanent, righteous life!

There is a great resurgence of interest today in the person and work of the Holy Spirit. People are becoming more and more aware of their personal needs and are seeking an addendum to just a "sweet by and by" message. Along with this they are seeing that the "trying to be holy" route is a dead-end street.

We do not obtain a relationship with the Holy Spirit by trying harder. He does not come to us through courageous self-effort or sincere religious achievement. He is ours by *faith*. God said so. "This is the only thing I want to find out from you: did you receive the Spirit by the works of the Law, or by hearing with faith?"[1] It is through God the Holy Spirit that we learn to succeed in Christianity without really trying. The issue is not trying but trusting.

We have talked about the limitless and people-centered love that God is. He loves us not through our merits, but through His. Because God loves us, He forgives us and makes us free.

But there is another step to His remaking us: He fills us. He literally comes to live within our human spirits by His Holy Spirit, and it is through the Spirit of God that we become one with Him and one with our brothers and sisters in the body of Christ. And though I believe these two onenesses are equally important — you can't have one without the other — it is upon the former that I choose to dwell here.

In Romans 8, which is generally regarded as a primary passage in the Scriptures on the Holy Spirit, Paul begins in verse one with a word of review just in case we have failed to catch his point thus far in his book: "There is therefore now no condemnation for those who are in Christ Jesus." God condemned His Son in our place on the cross, then raised Him from death, and elevated Him to the number one spot in all creation, at His right hand. And God sees us — all who trust in Him — as being *in* Christ. In other words, God views us just as He sees His Son.

Jesus will never again be under God's condemnation; He abides in His glory. What is true of Jesus Christ is true of us as His fellow heirs. We are *in* Christ. We are risen with Him to a new kind of life. And thus, we are not under the condemnation of God, nor will we ever be again! We are free from His wrath to rest in His love. He likes our program because we *are* His program. He's in this business of being God for our benefit, not just for His. From ages past, He has yearned for the day when He could be to us a God, and we could be to Him a people.[2] We're His kind of folks now. We're what He's all about, the object of His affection, the center of His attention. His day has come, through the Lord Jesus, and we are it!

Now, if the Father, because I am in Christ, does not condemn me, the question I need to ask is, "Why do I so often condemn *myself?*" Can't I learn to accept me as He does? Of course. Why should we be hung up on ourselves, when God isn't? If God doesn't condemn me, there is no reason why I should condemn myself. Am I better than He is?

It all goes back to this thing on the law. If I am living under the law, be it God's law or man's, I will constantly be engrossed in self-evaluation. But He has freed us from all that. Christ is the fulfillment of the law. And God tells us we are not condemned so He can get us out from under the stale dust of human achievement to simply count on Him to build His life within us.

"There is therefore now *no* condemnation . . . ." *God* doesn't condemn me, and *I* don't need to condemn me, either. And you can go a couple more steps. If I see myself as out from under the condemnation of God and of myself, I am free to no longer condemn others. This is the "how to" of what Jesus meant when He said, "Love your enemies,"[3] and "Forgive men for their transgressions."[4] If we see sin as dealt with in Christ, we have an outlook of forgiveness toward each other rather than an outlook of judgment.

Then, the last step in this progression is that we don't have to condemn God for what *He* does. This may sound silly, but sometimes I get short with Him. I'm angered by what He does to me. I got after Him one night when He sent some people over who needed to know Christ. I wanted to be alone with my family. I didn't like it. Naturally, as I look back, I wouldn't have had it any other way. He knew what He did was best not only for those people, but also for *me*. I needed that experience. And I love Him for it. That's why James says, "Consider it all joy, my brethren, when you encounter various trials; knowing that the testing of your faith produces endurance. And let endurance have its perfect result, that you may be perfect and complete, lacking in nothing."[5]

Life in the Holy Spirit keeps us from whatever we were before we knew God. We are released from the spiritual and mental results of transgressions of the past, and we are free from the law of sin itself; we never *have* to sin again.

If a person is not looking for anything, the odds are strong he won't find it. In looking for righteousness to spring up in us because we have the Holy Spirit within us, sin fades far into the background. In fact, the last half of the sentence just quoted from Romans 8:3 reads, "in order that the requirement of the law might be fulfilled in us, who do not walk according to the flesh, but according to the Spirit." The flip side of sin no longer being inevitable is that true righteousness in our lives and experience is *unavoidable* — if, as it says, we walk "according to the Spirit." His purpose, in this case, is to fulfill righteousness in us.

This is important: God does *not* fill us with the Holy Spirit to help us keep the law. Consciously or unconsciously, this is often what we come away with. "If I can just walk in the Spirit," we say to ourselves, "He will help me obey the Ten Commandments." No, it's better than that. Instead of telling us He will fill us so we can keep His law, God says because we have the Holy Spirit within us, He has already graded us A+ on law-keeping! In Christ, the righteousness of the law has been fulfilled. Therefore, instead of having to plug away to please Him, because of the Lord Jesus Christ the Father is already pleased. The pressure is off me to try to gain His favor.

As was mentioned in the last chapter, God still does issue orders. There are specific things He wants done by His people. These commands come our way from the Holy Spirit via the Lord Jesus Christ in a way not perceived through the five senses. For through a whisper of His Spirit, our Lord can mobilize His entire army. As we trust in and listen to the Lord, He will by His Spirit speak to us and lead us in the ways we are to go.

Let's look again at Romans 8, this time verses 5-9:

> 5. For those who are according to the flesh set their minds on the things of the flesh, but those who are according to the Spirit, the things of the Spirit.
> 6. For the mind set on the flesh is death, but the mind set on the Spirit is life and peace;
> 7. because the mind set on the flesh is hostile toward God; for it does not subject itself to the Law of God, for it is not even able to do so;
> 8. and those who are in the flesh cannot please God.
> 9. However you are not in the flesh but in the Spirit, if indeed the Spirit of God dwells in you. But if anyone does not have the Spirit of Christ, he does not belong to Him.

Two kinds of people are being described. There are those who are living in the flesh and those who are living by the Spirit. Look again at verse 9. If we understand that Paul is talking about those who have new life in Him as compared with those who don't, then the whole thing begins to fall into place.

One afternoon I was in Vancouver, British Columbia, teaching out of Romans 8 to a community of Christians who meet together in a home. The subject for the session had to do with the baptism and fullness of the Holy Spirit. As is often the case with me, I went a bit too long and overshot my time allotment.

When the meeting adjourned, I excused myself, stepped outside, and headed for my waiting car.

"Can I talk with you for a few minutes?" a young man asked, running up alongside me.

"I'm really sorry," I said, "but I'm already late to catch my plane at the airport."

"Well, how long would it take for the Lord to fill me with His Holy Spirit?" the student asked with a big grin.

"Oh, just a couple of seconds," I replied. I put down my briefcase, placed my hands upon his head, and prayed, "Lord Jesus, You know I'm out of time, so in the power of Your holy name I ask You to absolutely inundate this brother in the Holy Spirit. Right now. This instant. Thank You, Lord. Amen."

His smile was even wider. "That's it!" he said.

"When a person believes, it just takes God a moment or two to do His work," I said as I jumped inside the car.

There are so many of us on the loose today who are believing God with our heads but not our hearts. Science tells us nature seeks a vacuum. You know, I believe the same thing is true of the Holy Spirit. Without the fullness of His presence we are void and empty on the inside.

If you know Jesus Christ as your own, thank Him — in fact, why not take a moment and thank Him now — that the Holy Spirit is yours and ask Him to fill you. As has been said, "Faith is when you stop saying please and start saying thank you." Often we do not realize what God has given us until we take a moment and thank Him.

Not long ago I was reading the evening paper, and I noticed a story that had come over one of the wire services, which I believe originated in Boston. The bodies of two elderly spinsters had been discovered in their modest apartment. They had died a few days earlier. An autopsy revealed they had succumbed to malnutrition. The account went on to relate that later a search had been conducted in the apartment, and hidden in the mattresses and sewn up in pillows and draperies was nearly $200,000 in cash. Here were two people who possessed material abundance, yet they died in self-afflicted starvation.

We, as children of God, have been given the Holy Spirit. There is no reason at all for us to struggle to succeed in living with Christ, when God says the power for our new life is available in Him. We are rich in Christ. We are free to lay hold of this wealth and live all the way up to the brim and beyond.

Jesus said, "For where two or three have gathered together in My name, there I am in their midst."[7] This is the church in its simplest form. The Holy Spirit has not been given first to the individual; He has been given first to the church. This is not to say we cannot experience His fullness as persons. Whatever is true of the whole is true of the part. We are members or cells in the body of Christ, and since He lives in the entire body, He naturally indwells each cell. But the issue is this: it is not so much a matter of how I as a person can experience the reality of the Spirit, but rather how *we* as a *body* can enjoy His presence. Hearing a speaker once each week is fine, but it misses by a country mile what we are after here. That may teach us *about* God, but we need fellowship *with* Him, and He has so clearly indicated that fellowship with Him comes best in community. Else why would He have admonished us to frequently assemble ourselves together?[8]

Today, we have gotten away from this, but I believe God is bringing us around again. The *body* needs to function, not just a speaker within the body. We are accustomed to the whole body being a mouth! God desires, for our benefit and upbuilding, that all the members function.

In considering the element of time as related to the Holy Spirit, the Scriptures often speak of our walk in the Spirit. Our relationship with the Spirit of God operates on a continuum. Just as it would be inconceivable for God to pump the Holy Spirit in and out of the church, so it would make little sense for the Spirit to be on-again, off-again in our lives. It is interesting that Paul ascribes to the Lord the role of supplier of the Spirit, or, literally, "He who keeps on providing you with the Spirit."[9] It is God's job to keep His Spirit coming our way; all He desires on our part is that we rely upon Him to do so.

On the negative side, we often wonder if we quench or grieve the Spirit. Or, if we sin, will the Spirit depart from us. I feel we must return at this point to the opening verse of Romans 8, where we began. Sin has been judged at the cross. Or later in that same chapter, when Paul writes:

32. He who did not spare His own Son, but delivered Him up for us all, how will He not also with Him freely give us all things?
33. Who will bring a charge against God's elect? God is the one who justifies;
34. who is the one who condemns? Christ Jesus is He who died, yes, rather who was raised, who is at the right hand of God, who also intercedes for us.
35. Who shall separate us from the love of Christ? Shall tribulation, or distress, or persecution, or famine, or nakedness, or peril, or sword?

God wants us off this introspection kick. He wants us to trust Him. As we depend on Him for our forgiveness, for His love, for the provision of His Holy Spirit — not just alone, but with the fellowship of brothers and sisters in Christ — He will be real to us.

A child growing up can become a tragic personality cripple if he is constantly wondering if he has grieved his parents or if they are displeased with him. Part of the role of a mother or father is, because they love and adore the child, to teach him what kind of person he should be and how to live effectively.

So it is with God. If we have grieved or displeased Him, He will no doubt tap us on the shoulder and discipline (teach) us how to do it right. But it is *through* the Holy Spirit that He does this. That is a part of His leading in our lives. He does not give us over to ourselves the moment we spout off. He keeps us as His own.

We are educated by our superficial human, and even sometimes family, relationships to expect estrangement every time we do something wrong. If I lose a business deal, I expect the boss to be angry with me. If I make a poor showing in a classroom discussion, I am not surprised by a disappointed glare from my instructor. If I make a faux pas in high society, I can count on a cold shoulder from the elite. So naturally, when a person is tuned into the way the world runs, he expects God to withdraw from his presence if he sins.

I do not wish to sound like a broken record, but God says we're forgiven. We are accepted in the Beloved. So instead of falsely counting on breaking fellowship with Him, let's start counting on the "grace of the Lord Jesus Christ, and the love of God, and the fellowship of the Holy Spirit . . . ."[10] (Paul wrote *that* to the gross Corinthians!)

God says we are new people. He has planted within us new life. Old life looks at sin; new life looks at forgiveness. Old life is in fear; new life is in love. Old life expects estrangement; new life thrives on fellowship with God. Let's forget once and for all this emphasis on performance living and conditional love. It's time we learn to walk in confidence with God, expecting Him to use us, counting on Him to anoint us with power. If we should slip, let's trust the Savior and keep moving. He's taken care of all that.

This is what the world is waiting to see. People want something that works. We've been lifted far above this "up and down" kind of existence. We're seated in the heavenlies. God calls us overcomers — still meeting the problems that life offers, but overcomers. Winners! And the Holy Spirit within is the One who makes this life possible.

*Behold, how good and how pleasant it is for
brethren to dwell together in unity!*

Psalm 133:1

10. Where It All Takes Place

There is often a tendency for us to take the grace of God
(or any biblical truth) and attempt to live it out in faith on a
purely personal basis. Somehow the "Jesus and me" mentality, a stance significantly conspicuous in our twentieth century, has produced horrid Christian individualism on many
fronts. Today, many of us unknowingly have slumped
into a quasi-evangelical theology which says, "If I can, by
myself, make Jesus Christ Lord of my life, that's really all I
need."

Instead of living under the care and authoritative direction of
the body of Christ, we tend to view the church as the place we
stop in once or twice a week for an hour to get more teaching
and exhortation on how to keep on living our individualistic
Christian lives. In our zeal to preach that we are members of

111

Christil,[1] which is absolutely true, we have forgotten we are also members one of another.[2]

The place God designed for His unconditional love and forgiveness to be experienced is the church, as the body functions in power and vitality under the direction of the Holy Spirit. Some people get nervous at this point because of past experiences where being a church member has been made synonymous with being a Christian. And that's the *other* extreme! You see, God never planned for Lone Ranger Christianity which teaches all you need is just a *personal* relationship with Christ. Nor did He plan for churches where people become members without ever becoming born into God's family.

Jesus taught the wine *and* the wineskins,[3] the life and the container. Paul taught individual members *and* the body of Christ.[4] Or, to be allegorical for a moment, the cross is both vertical and horizontal. The Lord Jesus Christ is the mediator between God and man in our vertical relationship, and He is the bond of peace to bring unity and oneness between brothers and sisters in His church on the horizontal plane.

In his writings, Dr. Francis Schaeffer has made this point well: "God has made us in His own image, and He means for us to be in strong horizontal relationship with each other. While Christianity appeals and applies to the individual, it is not individualistic. God means for us to have community. There are really two orthodoxies: an orthodoxy of doctrine and an orthodoxy of community, and both go together."[5]

And it was so even in the Old Testament. You wouldn't have dreamed of being a believing Jew without being part and parcel of the nation of Israel. Can you imagine how Moses and Aaron would have responded to someone who said, "I want to believe in God, but let me establish myself under my own government —I'll sort of be an *arm* of Israel. But I don't want to be under your care at all. I get all the direction I need from God during my devotions each day." How the fur would have flown on that issue!

You see, the Holy Spirit has been given to us not to make us self-sufficient as Christians, but to distribute to us His gifts and ministries for our place of service in the body of Christ. In fact, listen to Augustine on that very matter: "A man who has the Holy Spirit is in the Church, which speaks the language of all men. Whoever is outside the Church has not the Holy Spirit."[6]

Augustine goes on to say, "If a part of the body is cut off. . . it retains the form of a finger, hand, arm, ear; but it has no life. Such is the state of a man separated from the Church. You inquire if he has the sacrament? He has. Baptism? He has it. The Creed? He has it. But what he has is merely the form. Unless you have the life of the Spirit, it is in vain to boast of the form."[7]

Or even earlier, Irenaeus, bishop of Lyons, who was taught by men taught by the Twelve, wrote, "For the Apostle says, 'God has set up in the Church Apostles, prophets, teachers, and all the other means of the Spirit's working. But they have no share in this Spirit who do not join in the activity of the Church. . . . For where the Church is, there is the Spirit of God; and where the Spirit of God is there is the Church and every kind of grace."[8]

FOREIGN AMBASSADORS

Suppose, for example, you and a close friend, both of you U. S. citizens, take a junket to Cairo, Egypt. During your stay in that city you meet a young man in his twenties who is there on a trip from Moscow. He is a citizen of the USSR.

The three of you start talking about your homelands over tea one afternoon, and you discover your Soviet friend is not only Marxist in his political doctrine, but is very dedicated to the Communist cause. Your feelings of Americanism are stirred as you begin to hear his views. You realize that even with its shortcomings and the sins of its people, democracy as a form of government is, to your way of thinking, vastly superior to communism. So the debate begins.

After four days you realize you are winning the first political argument of your life. This young Russian is coming over to your way of thought. By dinner time that evening, he actually renounces Marxism and embraces democracy! You are both shocked and elated. Who would have ever thought at the outset of your trip that you would witness a conversion from communism to democracy in Cairo? The young man had made a 180-degree turn philosophically.

As dessert is served, you say, "Well, we'd better start making some plans for you to move to America where you can experience what you've come to believe."

"No," your Russian friend says in his heavily accented English, "I have my roots back in Moscow."

You are crestfallen. "But you said that . . . ."

"Don't worry," he says, "you've convinced me. There's no way I'll slip back into Marxist thought. I'll get some of the classic books on the precepts of democracy as I travel through Europe on my way home. And I'm sure that in London or Frankfurt I can get a copy of the U. S. Constitution and maybe that Bill of Rights you talked about. I'll read and study daily to reinforce what you have taught me. But my home is Moscow."

You feel trapped. Sure, a person could continue embracing democracy in Moscow. But how would he ever flesh it out? He would be relating to democracy on a purely philosophical level, and nothing more. *No way could he experience citizenship.* (He would, however, subscribe to the Congressional Record!)

FREEDOM ON THE INSIDE

Listen, there's not a way in the world you can know the richness of God's grace, the joy of His love, and the freedom of His Holy Spirit apart from living as a citizen in a community of faith over which Jesus Christ rules as Lord. If you could experience God fully apart from the church, why on earth would Jesus have established it? The body of Christ is not optional. It's not an extra accessory to the gospel. The medium *is* part of the message! Enough of this mental religion which makes only *believers* and not *citizens* in the government of God!

Some may say, "But you told us earlier in the book that Christ has made us free. That He'll take us just as we are. That He has our best interest at heart. Can't I just let Him rule in my heart and not have to submit to His authority in some church?"

You can try it. But that is not the way it works. *Because* He has bought your freedom and has your best interest at heart, He gave birth to the church.

John 10 is a chapter about sheep and shepherds. Jesus said: "I am the good shepherd; the good shepherd lays down His life for the sheep. He who is a hireling . . . not the owner of the sheep, beholds the wolf coming, and leaves the sheep, and flees, and the wolf snatches them, and scatters them. He flees because he is a hireling, and is not concerned about the sheep."[9]

Where does a good shepherd keep his flock? Keeping them out in the woods or loose on the hillside does not work. Out there, they are open season for the wolves. Some will fall down into steep ravines and perish. So the caring shepherd builds a sheepfold. He fences in his property. Freedom, then, is *inside* the fence, where there are no wolves or ravines. Inside are green pastures and still waters. There, the flock finds safety and care.

So often, we have viewed freedom as jumping the fence. No, that's not freedom. It's rebellion. Freedom is where there's care and direction, not where the enemy abounds and the pitfalls are many. The latter are bondage of the first order. It is the citizens of God's government, secure inside the sheepfold, who are truly free.

BUT YOU DON'T KNOW MY CHURCH

There is a great dilemma which continues to confront us. It has to do, on the one hand, with seeing what the church is supposed to be, and, on the other hand, seeing it as it *is!*

People say, "They tell us to be under Christ's rule in the church. *But you don't know my church!* You couldn't experience God's love and forgiveness there if you tried. They've all but shut down the work of the Holy Spirit." And here the complaints are further complicated. Some say all they get is Bible doctrine with little warmth or compassion. Others say they receive a listening ear and human sensitivity, but little or no biblical teaching. Often you hear, "We're not even sure the minister is born again."

At this point the absolutely most frustrating question inevitably is asked, "How can we help to bring the church from where she is to where she needs to be?" And that question is further broken down into these: "Should I stay in and try to be a reformer? Should I move on to something better? Either way, what specific steps can be taken to improve things as they are?"

THE ROOTS OF ONENESS

To help us see what we're after, let's look back through history to the ancient church in its earliest years. From the very outset on the day of Pentecost, unity — oneness in the Spirit — was visibly present. Phrases like "together in one place,"[10] "of one heart and soul,"[11] and "for the common good"[12] were dominant throughout the apostles' writings. And, even when there were strong differences of opinion between persons or factions (see, for example, Acts 15:1-32, as the problem of legalism was dealt with; Galatians 2:11-16, where Paul got after Peter in no uncertain terms for playing footsie with false brethren; and most all of 1 Corinthians, where Paul nails factionalism and sins in general), the thought of the two parties going their separate ways was not entertained. They stayed together and solved their differences.

So strong was this oneness, that very early in its history the church came to be called "The One Holy Catholic and Apostolic Church." What a wealth of meaning in these words:

One. When we say the church was one, we do not mean geographically, for the church was soon scattered across the then-known world. Rather, as the Lord had prayed, "that they may all be one," [13] the body of Christ was one in authority, one in its confession of truth, and was unified by one Spirit.

This explains why Paul wrote midway through the first century, "There is one body and one Spirit, just as also you were called in one hope of your calling; one Lord, one faith, one baptism, one God and Father of all." [14] There was oneness in the sense of government: if, for example, you were put out of one church for habitual immorality, you could not walk down the street and join another. For there *was* no other church. Though there were many meeting places, the church itself was one.

Holy. To be holy means to be made righteous, to be set apart unto God. For it was He who said, "You shall be holy, for I am holy." [15] The church and its people were uniquely the property of the Father, Son, and Holy Spirit. So much so that the world tried to exterminate them. Secular authorities knew Christians belonged to another king and another kingdom, and the people were despised for their other-worldliness. In a day when the world is becoming churchier and the church is becoming worldlier, we would do well to reach back to the holiness of the early church.

Catholic. The ancient believers were catholic because they believed the same thing everywhere. There was a *universal* unity of faith, which is what the word *catholic* means. You did not hear one opinion on redemption in Jesus Christ in one town and another in the next town. They preached one gospel. It was difficult maintaining this catholicity, for heretics were present in those early years as they are today. But when differences arose, they were settled in council, and a major stream of belief and practice continued to be set forth and believed throughout the church.

Apostolic. The church was apostolic because it was built and served by men, called and gifted by the Lord Jesus Christ, who were the apostles, or the "sent ones." Most were uneducated, but with the Holy Spirit as their enabler they were well prepared, laying the foundations for the church with great precision and unselfishness.

What's more, that catholic doctrine had to be the doctrine of the original apostles. The "apostolic" checks the "catholic" and keeps it in line. And the church stayed on course when the initial apostles died. For they entrusted their message to faithful men who, in turn, were able "to teach others also."[16] New men, called and gifted by God, were constantly being raised up to transmit the truths of the Lord Jesus Christ which the Twelve had foundationally laid down.

Church. It was not only doctrine, but *people*, the "called out ones," established into communities drawn together as a new nation under the living government of God. These were more than Christian friends who sometimes made it out to fellowship meetings. These were people locked together in the love of Christ, the unity of the Spirit, cared for and served by the apostles and elders in the body of Christ. The name of the game was *church!*

Apostles followed apostles, and the church moved from the first century with men called bishops. Bishops in the mid-first century were evidently synonymous with elders; but by the late first and early second century, part of the apostolic role was taken by bishops who served the church and held her together.

There were bishops who possessed more responsibility than others. Those in larger cities came to have more respect.

THE FADING OF ONENESS

As things grew and expanded, successive bishops at Rome saw themselves as more important than other bishops, and finally saw themselves as heads of the church. By the sixth century, the gulf widened between the Eastern and Western church, and by A.D. 1054 all would agree there was a deep split. At least from this point on, there has not been a single universal church. The One Holy Catholic and Apostolic Church was a memory of the past as two bodies now laid claim to that title.

Along with this slippage in leadership and unity, the church slowly began to depart from the faith. Authority, worship, and doctrine were corrupted over those centuries, progressively more so until the time of the Reformation. You could still find true believers through those years, but the church as a whole was being lost.

Martin Luther and others wanted to *reform* the church, but Rome would not hear of it. Twice Luther approached the pope for a council and twice he was refused. And so came the great split of the Reformation. And splits have turned into splinters through the years which have followed.

In North America there *never has been* one church. Russia sent us its orthodox, Rome, its missionaries, England, its dissenters; *pluralism* became the calling card of the church on this continent. There wasn't even territorial unity — only pluralism. On our main intersections downtown, you could often find four different churches on each of the four corners — and be grateful that it wasn't a five or six corner intersection! People didn't even live near their places of worship. And with this pluralism, the sects and the heretics flourished.

With the coming of the nineteenth and twentieth centuries many "para-church" groups began, such as the YMCA,

YWCA, Inter-Varsity Christian Fellowship, Youth for Christ, and countless others. It was as though they were filling vacuums. As effective as some of these groups have been in their highly specialized areas, their very presence indicates the tragic loss of a valid ecclesiology on the part of the contemporary Christian public.

And in the last several years the "Christian seminar syndrome" has cropped up, taking us even further away from a recognized need for the church in its historic apostolic foundations. With much of conservative protestantism becoming, as Martin Marty has often dubbed it, "pop-evangelicalism"; liberalism dying on the vine; Anglicanism ordaining its first lesbian; Romanism continuing on as the world's largest denomination; and the Eastern church, while holding onto orthodox doctrine, experiencing few apparent breakouts of the power of the Holy Spirit, where does this all leave us? Is there any hope for the One Holy Catholic and Apostolic Church — the place where it all once happened — to get its act back together again?

The Twelve Commandments!

A short time ago that very question was asked among a group of seven of us who are involved in the "care and feeding" of churches. We asked, "What are the characteristics which today's church should strive to possess if it is to currently meet the needs of its people and show forth the glory of God in its unity?" There emerged from our meeting twelve key points.

1. *The Grace of God.* Since God deals with us in Christ according to His gracious, loving character, we need to be open receivers of this grace and reflect it in this world.

The church sorely needs to once again become a place where the love and forgiveness of God is shown forth, and cease being a center for legalistic condemnation. It seems to be almost a pattern that when Christian people are in trouble or hurting, "the last place we would ever want our problems known is in

our church." What a loss! For where else but among the people
of God can true compassion, acceptance, and healing be found
as they function by the grace and power of Jesus Christ?

2. *True Community.* The church of Jesus Christ must once
again be a people who are fully related to God and each other,
being vitally involved in all aspects of each other's lives.

We need to once again be *family* — people who belong to
and are related to one another. You can choose your friends,
but you can't choose your family! As living stones, we are set in
next to each other by the Holy Spirit. When we do not naturally fit, He has a way of chipping away at us — kindly — until
we do.

In true community we come to be each other's best friends.
We share our hearthsides, our tables; we learn to laugh together, cry together, and live out as a family the love of God
that has been shed abroad in our hearts. We are not the
isolated, private persons we once were. For the community of
saints is that special place where we share in real life forms the
total love of God!

3. *Vision.* The church in this century and the next needs to
reestablish its vision of the kingdom of God and true catholicity. It must be salt seasoning and a light shining in the darkness of a fallen world.

Each congregation in its own local and cultural setting must
be a living demonstration of the blessing and order of God's
reign, as contrasted with the confusion and anarchy of Satan in
a rebel world. The church must once again envision itself as
God's holy priesthood, interceding for an alienated world
which has turned its back on God, asking the loving heavenly
Father to receive back His prodigal creation. With a 20-20
vision, we can return our sights to laying hold of that for which
we were apprehended.

4. *An Authoritative, Serving Leadership.* The government
of each congregation should be carried out by an eldership

devoted to serving the people. Leaders in the church possess authority from God, and we the people respond obediently to their serving leadership.

How sorely we need elders who *eld* and bishops who *bish!* These are not merely men who occupy the front row on Sunday morning dressed in dark blue suits. They are shepherds of the sheep, people who give their very lives for those they serve and support.

5. *Care.* The Scriptures call those of us who are part of the body of Christ to look after the needs of our brothers and sisters in all areas of their lives. We need to view one another as total persons under the reign of Christ and relate to each other's needs in broad areas: financial, emotional, intellectual, vocational, as well as spiritual.

6. *Seeing and Hearing From God.* We need to learn once again to listen to the voice of the Holy Spirit as He speaks to us in the church. Too long have we merely followed "Christian principles" or directives God spoke to His people in years gone by.

As believers who walk in obedience to the Lord, having been baptized in the Holy Spirit, we should *expect* to hear from God. The church responds by judging the Word which is spoken, determining if it is true, and exhorting the people to obey what the Lord has said.[17]

7. *Good Works.* Faith without works is dead. Notice I did not say *dead works* (things done by human motivation, often to attempt to gain points with God or men), but rather *good works* (things done in direct response to the love of Christ as He speaks to and directs His people).

For the church, good works is putting its love for Christ and His people into action, person to person and collectively. We should expect God to be leading us into situations where we, for example, can preach the gospel to the poor, visit prisons and widows, care for the sick, and minister to people afflicted with other troubles. Our consciences have been cleansed from dead works to *serve the living God!*

8. *Godliness.* By godliness, we do not mean flashing syrupy smiles, being goody-goody, or maintaining an air of sloppy-agape. Godliness is having a belief that behaves, being citizens of the kingdom of God who follow His orders. As we live under the grace of God, we will show forth lives of love, moral purity, truth, kindness, justice, goodness, and similar characteristics to which God has always called His people.

9. *Orthodox Theology.* Much of the church today has lapsed into holding "fringe doctrine," teaching as fact novel views on prophecy, principles for living, renegade uses of spiritual gifts, and setting forth other interpretations of Scripture which have virtually no precedent in the believing church of history. From such, let us turn away! If the river of God's revelation is a hundred feet wide, let's go out fifty feet and head straight downstream!

May we once again hold to those doctrines which are based in Scripture, which are in keeping with the early councils and creeds of the church, and which have been commonly held by all communions of orthodox believers. The true church does not go after new or novel doctrines.

10. *Worship.* The heart of worship is praise to the Lord and thanksgiving to Him. The church once again must discover the forgotten art of making love to the Lord, joyfully and regularly gathering at the throne of God to worship the Father, Son, and Holy Spirit. Worship times need to be times where each member may participate, not where a multitude of spectators gape at a leader giving forth praise in proxy way up front.

11. *The Blessed Hope.* As members of His body, we look forward with great anticipation to the Second Advent of Christ the King and to participation in His forever kingdom which He will one day fully establish. We need to hear constantly that one day the kingdoms of the world which pester us and vie for

our allegiance will be judged, and there will emerge that new heaven and new earth conspicuously lacking in pain and sorrow. No wonder the beloved John said in response to seeing the glory of this hope, "Come, Lord Jesus!" [18]

12. *Catholicity.* As we have said, the church is divided. Never in history has division and sectarianism been the ideal of God. For this reason, the people of God long for the church to return to a state of unity which will say to the world, "Jesus is Lord."

WHERE DO WE GO FROM HERE?

Having said all this, how do we go about calling the church back to its roots?

The amazing thing to realize is that virtually all of us who name the name of Christ *want* the church to be one body again. Certainly there will be disagreement as to how this should be accomplished. But the basic desire is here. It is almost as though the church is waiting with expectancy for a new cadre of apostles and prophets to be raised up for us once again, to move with authority and power to set in order what is lacking.

Assuming, then, that we desire true catholicity and, even more important, that it is the will of God (which we know from the Scriptures), what are some positive steps which can be taken? See if some of these suggestions don't relate to the issue.

First, we need to discover again our historic mainstream doctrine. At this point, some super-spiritual saint will object, "Oh, but doctrine divides!" Not on your life. As a matter of fact, doctrine *unites*. It is only *false* doctrine which divides. So unity and catholicity demand we do our homework. And it's more than inductive Bible study — which sometimes can promote self-ultimate private interpretation of the Scriptures. We really do need to know what the fathers of the church taught as *they* interpreted the Scriptures. It's time to go back and dust off those early foundations, those early creeds, and see that there *was* unanimity of opinion in the major doctrines of the faith.

Second, the leadership of the church must once again learn to meet in council and together listen to the Lord speak. This, of course, means leaders must learn to say "uncle" and change when they are wrong. Face it, none of us would score 100 percent on a theology test if the Lord were to put one on us right now. But collectively, could the church come together, and were our people willing to bend, we would have a tremendous opportunity to interact on a conciliar basis and arrive at the common faith as revealed in the Scriptures. We must learn again to operate in council.

Third, the church will have to learn again to operate with the same form of government. (I can hear the moans and groans on this one!) For unity to be reborn, authority will have to once again be territorial, not denominational. Common government was one ingredient in the glue which held the ancient church together. And I believe I'm safe in saying just about all of us will have to say "uncle" on this issue of church government. Don't forget, most all churches today will tell you they operate on New Testament forms and principles. If that is so, why, when it comes to government, are we miles apart?

Fourth, the divisions in Christianity must be willing to lose their individual identities in order for a new identity under the Lordship of Christ to be gained. Some crow will have to be eaten here, too. But, you know, eating crow isn't quite so bad when you have others sharing the meal! We're all in this together.

Someone is bound to ask at this point, "Well, how about if we just love each other?" Look, that's been preached for decades, centuries. Certainly we need to love each other. But love is also something we *do*.

We've talked about the theology of love for nine chapters.

Now it's sleeve-rollin' time. Jesus said, "Greater love has no one than this, that one lay down his life for his friends."[19] He did it for us. If the church is ever to be one again, we'll need to start doing that for each other in the body of Christ.

I'll confess I'm really afraid deep down that unless we begin to repent of all our private and sectarian opinions and get it on with unity, God will once again call His sure-fire play for oneness: *persecution*. It's worked before.[20] And it will no doubt work again.

If you were God, what would you do? Would you watch your children scrap and snap at each other's heels all over the earth for the rest of time? Or would you step in and call a halt to this nonsense, with sternness and force if necessary? I know what I'd do — and it's because I love and cherish my children that I'd do it. Of course, we could just obey Him and avoid the hassle. . . .

For who is our hope or joy or crown of exulta-
tion? Is it not even you, in the presence of our
Lord Jesus at His coming? For you are our
glory and joy.   1 Thessalonians 2:19,20

11. Some Thoughts on Happiness

The University of Iowa is beautifully situated on the green rolling hills that border the Iowa River, which flows directly through the campus. The students are typically Midwestern — warm and friendly.

During a recent trip to that school, I was talking with a freshman in the student union. He had become a Christian the previous fall and was growing rapidly in his new faith.

"I really like this stuff I've been hearing on the love and grace of God," he said, as we sat down together over a Coke in the commons. "Right after I met the Lord, I got on this huge pressure binge of witnessing for Christ. I was told, either by words or inference, that it was necessary for my own growth and that God would really be pleased with me if I witnessed regularly. Naturally I did.

127

"When I began to understand that God's love for me was based on something far deeper and more permanent, I began to know a freedom in my life that I had never experienced before. I felt liberated from *having* to witness to everyone and from the guilt that followed if I didn't. I have grown far more since that time than in all the rest of my Christian life put together.

"There's only one hang-up," he went on. "I'm still not completely happy. I love to see people trust in Jesus Christ, but since I've gotten off this pressure thing, I haven't shared my faith a whole lot. Last fall I saw some action in my outreach; this spring I'm more at peace in my own heart, but there's still something missing. Know what I mean?"

I knew what he meant. I had been through it. It happens sometimes when we have lived for an extended period of time under the dictates of law and then suddenly break out into the pleasant atmosphere of God's grace. Rather than obeying the calls to action of the Holy Spirit, we respond more to circumstances as "how we feel" and get lost in spontaneous passivity.

At first, I was concerned as I saw this problem in my own experience and in the lives of others. But the cause for alarm has dwindled. After all, which is better — to walk by a program of forced works or to live by the power of the Holy Spirit, even though some major adjustments may be needed? I'll take the latter any day. And if our new walk really *is* in the power of the Spirit, not only will there be ultimately more works which result, but, just as important, the new works will be the real thing!

After a brief pause in the conversation, I looked up at my friend across the table. "What do you think it is that makes a free man genuinely happy?" I inquired, sensing that the Lord had given me that question to pose to him.

He looked puzzled. "I'm not really sure," he responded.

My thoughts started paging through notes and lectures filed

away in the closets of my memory to come up with something impressive and theologically profound. Then God reminded me to keep it simple. Simple? I wasn't even sure of the answer myself! "God is our Father, and we're His sons," I thought. "Maybe we can go with the father-son idea on a human level and arrive at a spiritual parallel."

"Dave," I said, "in an earthly, human relationship, what is it that makes a father happy with reference to his son?"

"I suppose when the kid obeys him," he replied.

Still fishing for the answer myself, I shot back, "But what if the kid obeys him grudgingly?"

"Then that wouldn't make him happy," Dave reasoned.

"I *am* a father," I thought to myself. "What is it in relation to my kids that makes *me* happy?"

Earlier that day, while driving from Chicago to Iowa City, I had stopped at a filling station for gas. While I was waiting inside the building for the attendant to service my car, I spotted a rack of children's toys nearby. Even though I made mental note that these guys were robbers in the prices they were asking, my attention was drawn to a small, metal gyroscope displayed along with the other items. I could practically hear my kids squeal if they had a chance to see it work. The thought of my own childhood bewilderment at seeing a gyroscope spin on a string or a pencil point came to my mind. I knew it was way overpriced, but I decided to go ahead and get it anyway, just because it would make them happy.

I related the incident to Dave. "Isn't the happiness of his children the thing that makes a father happy?" I asked.

"I guess it is," he replied slowly, still thinking the matter over in his mind.

"If that's true, and if the analogy holds," I said, "it must mean that God is happy when we are happy."

We both stopped talking and were silent. That seemed too simple. Sometimes, I think, we are so accustomed to the Word of God being presented negatively that when a bit of good news comes through to us, we tend to reject it and think, "Naw, God couldn't be *that* good." The thing we miss is that He is the actual *source* of goodness itself. How could man's standard for good ever be higher than His?

Part of the reason Jesus came to this planet was to give us true happiness. "These things I have spoken to you," Jesus said, "that My joy may be in you, and that your joy may be made full."[1] He wants us to be happy. And it gave Him great joy to be the one who cleansed us from sin. "Fixing our eyes on Jesus the author and perfecter of faith, who for the joy set before Him endured the cross . . . ."[2] Jesus Christ possessed great joy in dying for us, knowing that in the end our happiness would be complete. God is happy when we're happy, and we're happy when we know that God loves us, has completely forgiven us, and has placed us securely in the body of Christ.

So often, happiness is a memory of the past or a hope for the future. Many times we hear people express themselves whose basic attitude toward life is, "I wish the Lord would take me home." Or, just today someone said, "If only I could have lived in the times of Jesus." But what about *right now*? God loves you *now*. If your life were to improve 100 percent every day for the rest of your life, His love for you wouldn't increase one bit. God has given to you right now every ounce of love He possibly has in His possession. It is yours. And it gives God great joy to know that you and I are experiencing His joy, a product of His love.

Now, if God is pleased when we are happy, it would also follow that we will know true joy when we make others happy. So much of love is in giving. "By this the love of God was manifested in us, that God has sent His only begotten Son into the world so that we might live through Him."[3]

I have been tempted all my life to try to manipulate people. One writer put it this way: "God created us to love people and use things; our problem comes in loving things and using people." It was partly through realization of this vanity on my part that I came to trust in Christ. I had tried loving others in my own strength, and my strength gave out! I know of nothing that provides the human soul with more emptiness and frustration than the aftermath of exploitation. I think back to incidents in my own life when I was forced to live with myself after taking selfish advantage of another person. I would invariably ask myself, "Why did you do it?" but would never emerge with any answers. Even though I may have gained materially or egotistically through these incidents, I never came away happy.

What a contrast to living in the life and love of Jesus Christ. Instead of looking for ways others can benefit me, I am now free to look for ways I can benefit others. And in the life of love, you often do not get your way — but a heart of giving *does* make you happy. I guess that's why Francis of Assisi in understanding God's love for him could write:[4]

> Lord, make me an instrument of Thy peace.
> Where there is hatred let me sow love;
> Where there is injury, pardon;
> Where there is doubt, faith;
> Where there is despair, hope;
> Where there is darkness, light;
> Where there is sadness, joy.
>
> O Divine Master, grant that I may not so much seek
> To be consoled as to console;
> To be understood as to understand;
> To be loved as to love;
> For it is in giving that we receive;
> It is in pardoning that we are pardoned;
> It is in dying that we are born to eternal life.

Now, if it is through knowing Jesus Christ in His church that I can be made happy, it would stand to reason other people would be happy, too, living in that same atmosphere of God's love and forgiveness. In other words, since God is pleased when I'm happy, and I am pleased in making others happy, the best way in all the world to pass on to people our kind of joy is to introduce them to the serving reign of Christ in the community of faith.

John said as he wrote his first epistle, "And these things we write, so that our joy may be made complete."[5] Just having the opportunity to relate the good news about Jesus Christ to the people of God gave John great joy. It made his joy complete. I call it "running the joy cycle." Every time we have the chance in *any* way to flesh out the love of God to others, our joy cycle gets fulfilled all over again.

Further, just as I delight as a father in giving gifts to my children, so our heavenly Father delights in passing on the gifts of the Spirit to His family. As we come into the fullness of the Holy Spirit, He distributes His gracious gifts to us "just as He wills."[6] We, in turn, have something unique as persons to give to our brothers and sisters in the church — and to people out in the world as well — as we function as the priesthood of God. And it is in serving that we discover it *is* more blessed (literally, more *happy!*) to give than it is to receive.[7]

During that same week in Iowa I was speaking in a fraternity house one evening to a group of men and women from the university. As I was describing the love of God, I spotted a girl near the front of the group who was especially attentive. She seemed to hang on everything being said, and I knew God was conversing with her. After the meeting concluded, she was the first one to come up and talk to me. She introduced herself and said, "You will never know how much that helped me tonight."

"You accepted Jesus Christ tonight, didn't you?" I said.

Tears came into her eyes. "Yes, I did, a-and I'm s-s-so happy!" she blurted out.

I don't cry easily, but I became a bit choked up myself. "That makes me happy, too," I said enthusiastically.

And it really *did!*

A verbal stance for Christ isn't always the big deal we seem to make it — it's part of the total package. Very little is said in the New Testament with regard to firm commands to "get the word out." When you are in love, it's the natural thing to talk about it. Jesus did not say, "you must"; He said, "you shall."[8] Peter told a group of elders, "Shepherd the flock of God among you, not under compulsion, but voluntarily."[9]

A friend we have known for years is a business executive in Chicago. When he hires new management men for his firm, he brings in an industrial psychologist to help him screen his applicants. They will generally set aside several hours during a specific week for the appointments, and my friend sits in on these sessions to observe and evaluate while the consultant conducts the interview.

"We had men scheduled at different times all week," he told me. "I have never experienced a series of interviews like it."

When the first man was brought into his office, he said, the professional interviewer made sure the applicant was comfortably seated, and after introductions and appropriate greetings, the questioning began.

"He started out with all the easy ones like — where are you from? — married? — how many children? — what is your educational background? — until the guy was pretty near asleep. Then just as the man being interviewed was becoming confident, the consultant asked him, as if out of the blue, 'What is your purpose in life?'"

My friend described how the applicant was caught off guard and really had no answer. The interview, for all practical purposes, had terminated.

This technique of questioning continued all week. After each man was ushered in and seated in an easy chair, the opening questions would flow smoothly and the answers would come easily. Then, as the men would begin to relax, the target question would be posed.

Finally, as the week wore on, the last of the scheduled appointments arrived. As with the rest, he was introduced, warmly welcomed, and the interview was under way. After ten minutes or so of the easy questions, out it came.

"What is your purpose in life?" the interviewer demanded.

With hardly a moment's hesitation the man replied, "My purpose in life is to have eternal life and to take as many people with me as possible!"

This time, too, the interview, for all practical purposes, was ended. The one conducting the questions was so caught by surprise that he had few questions left to ask.

Here was a man in the business world, not being paid to say one word about spiritual life, who expressed a reason to live which far outstripped the man who was the seeming expert on how to live!

If our Christianity is a programed set of rules and activities, we are certain candidates for spiritual fatigue and waning interest. But if we catch the life of Christ as it really is and operate as members of His body in the context of the special gifts He has given us from His Spirit, knowing Him becomes more creative and rewarding each day. We have a God who shows up and who abides with His people continually with a compassion and concern that never quits.

*Behold, I will do a new thing; now it shall
spring forth.*   Isaiah 43:19

12. Love Is Now

The thought has come to mind at times, "Do I really *understand* completely all these things about God's love and grace?" Over and over again, my assurance has been that regardless of whether or not I understand analytically, I am *in* His love and His grace because I am in Him. God Himself says that His love is beyond intellectual comprehension;[1] the amazing thing is because of Jesus Christ His love is wonderfully within the possession range of our experience.

A great and subtle tendency for me is to attempt to grow in doctrine alone, and not to grow in Christ and His kingdom. A system of thought is a much more convenient method of understanding, a far more natural atmosphere to our human life, than is knowing the person of Christ Himself. For it is He who is our life. It is He who lives, not words about Him. "The letter kills, but the Spirit gives life."[2]

In my own experience, I needed to know that all my sins were forgiven at Calvary, once-for-all, because an incomplete awareness of God's forgiveness kept me shielded from a receptive and living confidence before Him. Knowing the love of God has changed my very being because knowing His love has allowed me to accept myself, others, and even Him in a brand-new way. Knowing my freedom in Jesus has permitted me an escape from the limitations of old, mechanical motions that have always been such an integral part of my life and perspective.

I no longer see myself as a machine of God, but as a man of God. He is not interested in me first as a vessel or an instrument, but first as a person. Therefore, when He says that He fills me with the Holy Spirit, I see a real-life individual as the possessor of that Spirit, and not an impersonal conduit. His Spirit is not within like the blinking light of a neon sign, on-again and off-again; instead, He is in me as *life*. By His matchless Holy Spirit I am wed to Him and to the body of His Son in a living way, a way that is permanent and consistent.

His Spirit does not yank and pull Himself from me only to return again to potentially depart, any more than I would continually divorce myself from my wife but keep on coming back. That is not relationship; it is reaction. Love *acts* rather than *reacts*. God is active in our behalf, and He has taken up residence in the hearts of all who welcome Him. And He dwells in the midst of His people.

The reason that forgiveness, undemanding love, freedom, and all the rest have made such a personal impact is that through the new vision of these manifestations of Jesus Christ the debris of legalism, fear, self-condemnation, and formula-living has been swept aside and discarded. In a sense I have begun all over again to be unencumbered by mechanical "religion," to know Jesus Christ as I did when I began with Him years ago. My goal is not to garner new insights into forgiveness as such; it is to know Him. I do not wish to pursue the theological intricacies of how freedom works or to apply new principles of the ministry of the Holy Spirit so that I may better contain Him. My desire is to walk with Jesus Christ and His people.

In responding to the power of Simon Peter's life the religious authorities did not say they felt he knew a lot about Jesus, for they had already perceived Peter and his cohorts were ignorant and unlearned men. They saw that these men had been *with* Jesus.[3] He was a very part of them. People did not approach the apostles and say, "We desire to grasp more fully the teachings of your Savior." They said to Philip, "Sir, we wish to see Jesus."[4] Facts about "light" are not the issue, for "In Him was life; and the life was the light of men."[5]

God craves us for Himself at whatever point we may be at this instant! He loves us right now. Love is now because God is now. He is not waiting for us to change — He will tell us which changes need to be made and will empower us to make them. He will not tarry for lack of understanding, for He brings with Him understanding. He wants to impart *Himself* to us. And He wants to do it *now*.

There is another tendency I have found in my life pattern that limits the thrust of our God. And that has been to turn to the Scriptures, to prayer, and to the Word alone. *Alone*. There is no more empty word in my vocabulary than *alone*. Certainly, I will learn of Him and feast upon His love in the silence and solitude of my private chambers. As we spend quiet hours together in secret, He will unveil Himself to me in a new array of loveliness.

But it is in His body where Jesus dwells. That was true during His physical life on earth, and it is equally true during the reign of the Holy Spirit in the church. And I do not mean an ethereal, make-believe life. I mean the life Christ lives in us today through the Holy Spirit. God's Spirit has been sent to the church, the body, and not as "many" Holy Spirits to individual upon individual. We know and experience the Lord Jesus best as we know Him through His body.

If you receive a picture and a letter from a new acquaintance, you can know him on a limited basis that way. But seeing him in person and being with him allows you a far greater opportunity for fellowship and unity.

Jesus is best known in person. Since it may be awhile before we go to Him, He has agreed to come to us. He is present today in His body. Most people are! But His body is different from our own. We possess individual bodies; His body is corporate. It is composed of all who trust Him. And you and I will never know optimal oneness with Him in this life unless we know oneness with Him through others.

Do you tire of being a loner spiritually, as I do? I pray that you do. His love right now is ours through something far beyond our peronal relationship with Him. His love is ours through a corporate relationship with Him as well.

Finally, whether we like to admit it or not, we lean toward becoming products of our environment. That is one reason Paul told the Romans, "Do not be conformed to this world,"[6] or as J. B. Phillips translates it, "Don't let the world around you squeeze you into its own mould."[7] Ours is an age of specialization. In formal education we are learning more and more about less and less. From its industrial beginnings, for example, the automobile has evolved from a "horseless carriage" to a complex transport device. No longer capable of being serviced just by a mechanic, we now need transmission specialists, front end specialists, and another whole new team to repair the air conditioner. In the same way, we rarely employ one group of men to build a home. Today we contract separately for the plumber, the electrician, the interior designer, and on and on.

This same philosophy of specialization has carried over into the spiritual realm as well. In the beginning there was the church. Today there is the church, plus. We have training

centers or seminaries, evangelistic organizations, welfare
agencies, Christian political movements, and even people who
write Christian books!

A result of this spiritual smorgasbord of available goods and
services is that each one pushes "his own thing." Each group
emphasizes its own distinctive or specialty. And unfortunately
the whole business comes through to us in such a way that we
begin to think that unless we have tasted a portion of what each
specialty house has to offer, there is no way to enjoy victory in
the Christian life. By implication, joy with Christ is always
another Bible conference, Christian book, or theological insight away.

The "soul-winner" says that until we master his technique
and give our lives to witnessing, we will be unfulfilled. The
"personal devotions" proponent says that the deepening of
one's life in the Word is the final answer to personal need.
Renewal comes, says the specialist in "small groups," when
people come together in the environment of honesty and
quest. One who has experienced a "spiritual gift" claims a new
dimension of depth and satisfaction, and often views others as
missing out unless they obtain his gift.

Where does God fit into all of this? And how does Joe
Christian come to know the simplicity of Jesus Christ and His
church when, just as he thinks he's found the final missing link
to his faith, somebody else comes along and says, "Here, try
my shortcut."

Not only is God in love with us where we are, but He wants
us to be in love with Him where He is, too. Certainly, if you or I
need something further in our Christian experience, we can
trust Him (if we can trust *anybody*) to give it to us, and more.
"If you then, being evil, know how to give good gifts to your
children, how much more shall your Father who is in heaven
give what is good to those who ask Him!"[8] Jesus Christ will not
ever withhold from us one single thing that we need to have

victory in Him as we walk as citizens of His kingdom.

Men and movements, yes, even those who write books, will tell you they have the secret to victory and joy in Christ. Make sure when you listen that the "secret" is Jesus and not another activity, law, goal, strategy, or something else. Imagine the apostle Paul coming along with a line like this: "Until you've experienced all that I have experienced, there is no way to enjoy a consistent Christian life." Could *any* of us ever have a chance to experience all that he had seen and heard and done? Experiences come from Jesus Christ; Jesus Christ does not come from experiences. And we experience His lordship or headship in the church; He is author and perfecter of our faith.

"As you therefore have received Christ Jesus the Lord, so walk in Him, having been firmly rooted and now being built up in Him and established in your faith."[9] We, as living stones, are *now being* built up together in Him. The Lord is our Shepherd; as His flock, we are promised we shall not want. And He loves us now, for love is now, and God is love!

Notes

CHAPTER 1

[1]John 10:10 (KJV).
[2]George Whitefield, *Journals* (London: Banner of Truth, 1960), p. 209.

CHAPTER 2

[1]Ephesians 2:8-10.
[2]1 Corinthians 15:3.
[3]Hebrews 10:10; Ephesians 1:7; Romans 4:7-8.
[4]Hebrews 10:14.
[5]Isaiah 55:8-9.
[6]Romans 8:1-2; Romans 6:22; 2 Corinthians 5:17.
[7]Micah 7:19.
[8]Psalm 103:12.
[9]Isaiah 44:22.
[10]James 2:10.
[11]Romans 8:1.
[12]Hebrews 6:10.
[13]2 Peter 1:9.
[14]Luke 7:48.

CHAPTER 3

[1]Romans 5:8.
[2]I am using the account in Luke 7:36-50.
[3]Luke 7:40-42.
[4]1 Samuel 16:7.
[5]Luke 7:44-46.
[6]Proverbs 7:17.
[7]Luke 7:47.
[8]S. I. McMillen, *None of These Diseases* (Westwood: Fleming H. Revell, 1963), p. 116.
[9]Ezekiel 18:4.
[10]Romans 6:23.
[11]1 Peter 1:16 (KJV).
[12]Jude 24; Colossians 1:22.
[13]Compare Genesis 22:8 with John 1:29.
[14]Micah 7:18.

CHAPTER 4

[1]For a clear discussion of gnosticism, see *The International Standard Bible Encyclopaedia*, Volume II (Grand Rapids: Eerdmans, 1939), pp. 1240-1248.
[2]Ephesians 5:8.
[3]1 John 2:12.

CHAPTER 5

[1]1 John 4:19 (KJV).
[2]Ephesians 4:15.
[3]Romans 5:7-8.
[4]Isaiah 59:2.
[5]Hebrews 9:7.
[6]1 John 4:18.

CHAPTER 6

[1]Romans 2:4.
[2]Luke 15:11-32.
[3]Luke 15:20.
[4]John 5:24.
[5]John 19:30.
[6]John 3:36.
[7]2 Corinthians 5:19.
[8]Psalms 32:1-2; 130:3.
[9]Hebrews 8:12.
[10]Philippians 4:13.
[11]2 Peter 1:3.
[12]Hebrews 13:5.

CHAPTER 7

[1]1 John 4:19.
[2]Mark 12:31.
[3]Ephesians 5:28.
[4]2 Timothy 2:21.
[5]1 Corinthians 6:11.
[6]Revelation 1:6.
[7]Ephesians 2:10.

CHAPTER 8

[1]Hebrews 8:13.

[2]Hebrews 8:10.
[3]1 Corinthians 15:56.
[4]Galatians 3:24.
[5]2 Corinthians 3:3.
[6]Psalm 37:4.
[7]John 10:10.
[8]John 8:32.
[9]2 Corinthians 3:17.

CHAPTER 9

[1]Galatians 3:2.
[2]Jeremiah 31:33.
[3]Matthew 5:44.
[4]Matthew 6:14.
[5]James 1:2-4.
[6]1 John 2:1.
[7]Matthew 18:20.
[8]Hebrews 10:25.
[9]Galatians 3:5.
[10]2 Corinthians 13:14.

CHAPTER 10

[1]1 Corinthians 6:15; 12:27; Ephesians 5:30.
[2]Romans 12:5; Ephesians 4:25.
[3]Matthew 9:17; Mark 2:22; Luke 5:37-38.
[4]1 Corinthians 12:27.
[5]Francis A. Schaeffer, *The New Super Spirituality* (Downers Grove, Ill.: InterVarsity Press, 1972), p. 6.
[6]Henry Bettenson, *The Later Christian Fathers* (London: Oxford University Press, 1970), p. 237.
[7]Ibid.
[8]Henry Bettenson, *The Early Christian Fathers* (London: Oxford University Press, 1956), p. 83.
[9]John 10:11-13.
[10]Acts 2:1.
[11]Acts 4:32.
[12]1 Corinthians 12:7.
[13]John 17:21.
[14]Ephesians 4:4-6.
[15]1 Peter 1:16.
[16]See 2 Timothy 2:2.
[17]See 1 Corinthians 14:29-31.

[18]Revelation 22:20.
[19]John 15:13.
[20]For an interesting study on how persecution strengthens unity, consider Acts 4:23-35.

CHAPTER 11

[1]John 15:11.
[2]Hebrews 12:2.
[3]1 John 4:9.
[4]This is the famous "Prayer of St. Francis" and is found, among other places, in Maria Sticco, *The Peace of St. Francis* (New York: Hawthorne Books, Inc., 1962), p. 285.
[5]1 John 1:4.
[6]1 Corinthians 12:11.
[7]Acts 20:35.
[8]Acts 1:8.
[9]1 Peter 5:2.

CHAPTER 12

[1]Ephesians 3:19.
[2]2 Corinthians 3:6.
[3]Acts 4:13.
[4]John 12:21.
[5]John 1:4.
[6]Romans 12:2.
[7]J. B. Phillips, *The New Testament in Modern English* (New York: Macmillan, 1959), p. 332.
[8]Matthew 7:11.
[9]Colossians 2:6-7.